A PASSION FOR
COLLECTING

DECORATING WITH YOUR FAVORITE OBJECTS

A PASSION FOR
COLLECTING

Caroline Clifton-Mogg

photography by Simon Upton

Bulfinch Press
AOL Time Warner Book Group
Boston New York London

In memory of Anna, a great collector

First United States Edition

First published 2002 by Jacqui Small
An imprint of Aurum Press Ltd

ISBN 0-8212-2778-5
Library of Congress Control Number 2002107834

Bulfinch Press is a division of AOL Time Warner Book Group

Printed and bound in China

3 0966 00085 7512

CONTENTS

COLLECTING INSTINCTS

Everyone knows someone who collects something, whether it is as small as, say, china figures or as large as wall-sized works of contemporary art. We respond to collectors and their collections with an instinctive interest, to the extent that what they collect is very often the first thing we remember about new acquaintances.

Perhaps it is born in us to collect? Some might say so, and certainly for many children, their "collection" is often the most precious thing in their possession. They may hoard marbles and toy soldiers, postage stamps or shells, but whatever the particular treasures, who does not remember the thrill in the arranging, sorting, selecting, and admiring of your possessions? And in the hunt, always hoping to find the next and better prize? But perhaps the collecting instinct is not allied just to childhood experiences, but more to a general nostalgia – for childhood pastimes, of course, but also for other memorable times in our lives; for places, people, and events when we were happy. This may explain why so many people prefer to collect things that have associations with the past rather than the present.

Above left *Charles Paget Wade's home in England remains a collector's dream. During the 1930s, he was particularly interested in gathering the crafts of the English countryside; here, in the Priest's House, is a collection of kitchen artifacts.*

Top right *David Gill is a collector for whom every object, whether large or small, is to be treasured. He mixes old with new and ornate with simple, with studied abandon.*

Above right *In this composition of color and patina, animal skulls and a snake's head are combined with religious objects, grounded by a pair of verdigris metal lamp bases and a watered green background.*

Top right *Objects that have little in common other than a certain color and texture can, with skill, be made into a collection as easily as a group of uniform silver matchboxes.*

Above right *In the Gropius house, each piece of furniture, such as this desk he designed for his own use in the Weimar Bauhaus, becomes an integral part of the collection of the objects that make up a home.*

Above far right *The Portland Vase, a Wedgwood version of which stands in the center of the bottom shelf, was a source of inspiration for nineteenth-century ceramic design, as the two pots left and right of the upper shelf illustrate.*

A PASSIONATE OCCUPATION

A true collector is there for the chase, the anticipation, and the satisfaction of possession. Collecting is about passion, about tracking down the perfect object to enhance your life – and then re-entering the race and continuing the search for the next perfect piece. And the collector is always persistent in his hunt, although perhaps not all are quite so dogged as the great American early twentieth-century collector, J. Pierpont Morgan. Trying to buy the Lord Byron manuscripts, owned by a relative of Byron's in Greece, Morgan hired a man, gave him a letter of credit, and sent him to live in Greece, where he remained for several years, until he had finally bought all the manuscripts. Collecting the best that the world has to offer of art and antiquities has, in fact, long been a pastime undertaken by men with the wealth and the education to do so. Documented collections have been recorded since the early Renaissance; both in Italy and other European countries, the noble and wealthy were acquiring antique sculpture and forming libraries of great worth. The eighteenth century was

perhaps the Golden Age of the collector, and many had catholic tastes and enough money to indulge them, buying anything that took their fancy and putting it on display in their cabinets and galleries.

Collecting is a kind of contagious virus that, once contracted, rarely leaves the infected person. The symptoms may lie dormant for a time, but the disease usually recurs – often with renewed vigor. There can be a certain snobbery about collectors and collecting, an idea that one discipline or area is more "important" than another or that it is amateur to collect too many different things. I personally think that once a collector, always a collector, and I warm to a man like Sir William Hamilton, British envoy to Naples in the 1700s, who was widely respected as an authority on classical antiquities. He built up not just one collection, but two, selling the first and immediately beginning to assemble the second. It included the same type of fine Etruscan vases and other important pieces that he had amassed the first time around, but Hamilton could not resist buying and cataloguing additional classical inconsequentials. He collected, for example, the head of a bodkin, fragments of horses' harnesses, a Roman foot-rule, and fourteen bronze dice. He was following a worthy tradition; seventeenth-century diarist John Evelyn records a Venetian collector of 1645, whose possession of a brass nail found in Nero's golden house filled him with as much excitement as all his far more important pieces. That is the mark of a true collector – the fact that he or she is never willing to let anything pass by, as it may, after all, be important some day and is in any case interesting now.

What is "interesting" as opposed to merely rare or beautiful is, of course, open to many interpretations, but often has to do with the intimate and the practical – the stuff of daily life, rather than the set pieces. There have long been as many who are interested in the way people actually lived as they are in the works of art they created, and collecting everyday objects seems to give an insight into other lives that a fine painting or handpainted set of china cannot suggest. Our modern interest in seeing the working of heritage homes – the equipment in the kitchens and laundry rooms, as well as the fine furniture and furnishings of the receiving rooms – is perhaps a contemporary manifestation of the same instinct.

THE CHARACTER OF A COLLECTOR

This book explores the phenomenon of collecting, looking in detail at some of the areas collected – some obvious, some less so – and at some of the personalities behind the collections.

Below *In Jerry and Susan Lauren's Manhattan apartment, a nineteenth-century weather-vane in the form of a horse is displayed in close juxtaposition with a picture by American painter, Bill Trailer.*

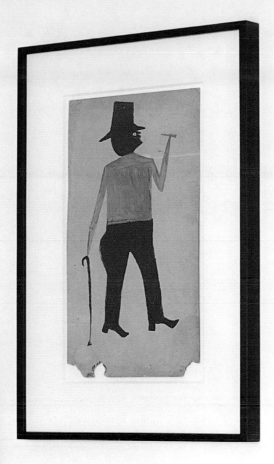

We also study the art of displaying a collection, whether it is of rolling pins or rolled gold, showing every collection in a way that is both attractive and inspiring to others.

We have divided the collectors and collections into nine loose groups. There are the Antiquarians, direct descendants of those Renaissance and eighteenth-century collectors, although we didn't find any quite so involved as Hippolito Vitellesco, visited in Rome in 1644 by John Evelyn. "Hence we went to the house of Hippolito Vitellesco," Evelyn records, "who shew'd us one of the best collections of statues in Rome, to which he frequently talkes as if they were living, pronouncing now and then orations, sentences and verses, sometimes kissing and embracing them."

The Explorers are exemplified as those who collect ethnic and other curiosities from all over the world, while the Inheritors are those who receive wholesale either an existing collection or the idea of one. The Perfectionists are collectors who only want the best in its field – whatever their definition of perfect be. Then there are the Naturalists – those drawn to objects from the natural world, whether minerals, flora, or fauna. The Utilitarians encompass all those collectors who see the beauty of the practical and the workaday; and the Enthusiasts are those all-round collectors who cannot resist scooping up everything that appeals to them, from books to banjos. They are the descendants of all those owners of teeming cabinets of curiosities who so enjoyed the charm of the small. The Decorators are those talented people who

Left *In the apartment of legendary New York decorators Zajac and Callahan, an unusual collection of mirrors radiates and reflects an eclectic treasure house of decorative objects, uniting everything in the room into a homogeneous whole.*

Right *French collectors Franck Delmarcelle and Laurent Dombrowicz display their religious art and reliquaries in combination with an assortment of other like-minded objects, concentrating on the correct elements of scale and balance.*

Above right *The sharp polished planes of these fine, small nineteenth-century bronzes by Alfred Gilbert and Reynold-Stephens are set off perfectly by the glowing wooden surface of the table and the rich cerulean blue of the wall behind.*

Below right *One of the best ways to pull together and make a collection from a disparate group of objects is to unite them with color – in this case, the perennial combination of black and white.*

Far right *Everything about this group is of a natural piece: the small, simple model boats are shown together on a rough-hewn surface, against a painted background that evokes a sense of sea and sky.*

Above *Seen individually, these bronze insects and reptiles might almost be too small to be immediately noticed, but when they are grouped together in an almost creepily realistic way, and arranged in front of cream-glazed ceramics, they command instant, careful attention.*

collect objects that, while worthy in themselves, also have the ability to transform any space with their decorative essences. Finally, the Miniaturists are fascinated by the minute – whether it is tiny paintings, medallions, boxes, or ceramic pieces.

These categories are not as arbitrary as they might at first seem, for although all collectors are similar in their love of their particular subject, they are also all different. Each one collects in a way that reflects their personality and their day-to-day lives. There are some collectors who resolutely concentrate on one type of object and are not

deflected until that specific collection is – in their eyes – complete, such as Susan and Jerry Lauren, with their first-rate American weathervanes and associated American artifacts. Then there are others who start with one thing, but along the way find side roads, wide avenues, and even cul-de-sacs, down which they must duck and dive while they become ever more knowledgeable. Many early collectors were of this persuasion, and here Paul Dawson and Harold Galloway are examples, as they have expanded their collection as they learned more and more about Victorian art and associated crafts.

Then there are the fastidious, the careful, who do not collect haphazardly, but choose each addition for its aesthetic quality or provenance. Polly Dickens, an English collector living in the United States who collects ceramics and glass, is a fine example. Each piece, although intrinsically simple, is very carefully chosen for precisely the right lines and shape, and then carefully arranged so that its virtues and simple beauty may be appreciated. The happy-go-lucky person has an entirely different approach: for him or her the world is one giant collection waiting to be raided for collections of the old, the useful, the useless, and the precious. Such a collector likes the quirky and the eccentric, has a story about everything, and loves each piece as much as the next – sometimes to the bafflement of everybody else.

FOR LOVE, NOT MONEY

There are those who collect as an investment, although not as many as you would think; in fact, in most cases the investment opportunity is almost incidental. This is probably just as well, since – certainly at the present day – art is not usually as good an investment as money put into other traditional areas, such as stocks and shares or property. We have all read the stories of pieces bought for a song being sold for a fortune, but for every hitherto unappreciated treasure, there are many, many objects bought for what was a high price and which have failed to rise accordingly. Although through the cloud of time it seems as if everyone in former centuries collected things of great worth, buying them for a song, many were bought at more than their

Above *The scale of a collection and the way in which it enhances its surroundings is important. In this lofty, beamed country dining room, the pieces on display – that are as varied as angels and urns – more than hold their own displayed against the architecture.*

Below *Another exercise in scale – this time in miniature – is to be found in designer Hubert Zandberg's small apartment, which is skillfully filled with the fruits of his collecting. The underlying theme of natural life ties all the various objects artistically together.*

Above *In the Manhattan apartment of Reed Krakoff, master of the careful edit, an understanding of scale is again evident. Here, a striking artwork by Friedel Dzubas is carefully chosen to live harmoniously with the understated furniture.*

Right *Relatively small objects on a table must be put together with an even more acute sense of scale and balance than when arranging larger pieces. This is a most careful composition, complete with nautilus shells, worthy of a seventeenth-century still-life painting.*

then market value. William Beckford, for one, was well known for paying above the odds for an object that he really desired – and he could well afford to do so. What people collect has always been susceptible to whim, and made desirable through the interests and fashions of the day. Although it may be true that a collection – several examples of a genre – is usually worth more when it is sold than a single example, most contemporary collectors, even if they started with the idea of investment opportunity, generally become hooked on the joy of the objects themselves.

Late nineteenth-century America provides spectacular examples of collecting fever. It was a time of great expansion and, for some, great wealth. By the late 1800s, some parts of New York – 5th Avenue in particular – looked as if the stones

Left *This room in Gropius's Massachusetts house is a microcosm of the history of contemporary European design between 1920 and 1940. Almost all the furniture in this living and dining room was made by Marcel Breuer.*

Right *In contrast, this wall displaying Victorian decorative art, in the form of nature tableaux and related artifacts, could be described as a microcosm of the nineteenth-century passion for nature study and classification.*

of the chateaux of the Loire Valley had been tossed into the air, placed in a compactor, and dumped across the Atlantic. Many of the new millionaires built there, including several members of the Vanderbilt family, and nearly all collected to some degree – if only to have enough to fill their new mansions in the manner in which they felt they ought to learn to be accustomed. Their spiritual leader was undoubtedly the banker, J. Pierpont Morgan, who amassed an enormous fortune, much of which he spent on acquiring art objects on a grand scale. These were later to become one of the greatest collections of the early twentieth century. Many of his pictures and works of art now form the core of the collection of the Metropolitan Museum in New York, and others can be seen in the Pierpont Morgan Library, which he built for himself in 1900.

During the twentieth century, Americans continued to dominate the high-spending end of the collecting world, with men such as Henry Clay Frick, who later bought five of Morgan's fourteen paintings by Fragonard; Andrew Mellon, who was once valued at fifty million; and Louis Bache, valued at a mere

twenty million. Many of the works that they were persuaded to buy were exported from Europe by the clever and successful English dealer Joseph Duveen. Like an agent of the aristocracy in the seventeenth and eighteenth centuries, Duveen dominated the market and bought single artworks and entire collections of the very highest quality, and then sold them on at a considerable premium to the rich collectors of the day. But others collected, too, albeit on a more modest scale. As the twentieth century progressed, in England more "antiquity" shops, as they were then known, opened, and newspapers and magazines devoted more space to articles about collecting. Auction houses played a more and more important role in the acquisition and dispersal of desirable objects.

Fashions change in collecting as much as in any other area of taste. As has always happened, many people tend to collect the new pictorial art of their time, such as photography, cartoons, or holograms. Then sources and supplies dry up, so new areas must be searched out, often by auction houses, who try to identify new areas where they can establish a market. There sometimes seem to be communal, inexplicable passions for groups of objects, maybe in areas that have been neglected and which are therefore easily found at good prices; or in others in which people seem to take an almost perverse enjoyment in pursuing. An early twentieth-century book on collecting, for example, devotes separate chapters to such arcane collectibles as old deeds, trader's tokens (a form of bartering chip), straw marquetry, and decanter labels. Ever more categories seem to be desired by someone: a recent magazine article extols the fun to be had in collecting coat hangers (yes, really); and one dealer specializes in early light bulbs. It just goes to show that there is a home, and a collector, for everything.

In the end, though, a collection is probably one of the most individual statements that a person can make, relatively untouched by fashion or contemporary enthusiasms; it is a listing of interests and lifestyle, an examination of character and concerns. As arch present-day collector Vicente Wolf says: "A collection speaks volumes about the person who created it – how artistic you are, how creative, how well travelled and well read, whether you have a sense of humor or perversity and how far you stray from the way other people think of you. It shows what your sense of balance and scale is, but most of all it shows who is behind the façade." Collections directly reveal the personalities behind them.

One cannot but warm to collectors as an identifiable group. How could you fail to like people who are so different in one way – loving such diverse things as shells, bones, cups, candlesticks, chairs, colored glass, weathervanes, and broken mirrors – and yet are all, without exception, constantly curious, constantly excited about the past and about the present world around us? Collecting may be characterized as a form of self-indulgence, but it is one that is generally inclusive – a club that welcomes new members with great enthusiasm. Collectors are what they are because as a pursuit, a pastime, a way of life even, their activity is surprising, interesting, educational, and, above all, always fun.

Above right *Everywhere you look, there is something interesting in this careful monochrome composition, based around a fine seventeenth-century Italian ivory and ebony cabinet. There is an underlying theme of neo-classicism, and its influence and discipline is apparent throughout the group.*

Above far right *No-color colors are used to make a homogenous group of a selection of family photographs, pictures and objects. Below, the fireplace acts as a frame for a striking oversized white dish.*

Below right *It may look easy, but it takes skill to combine collections as diverse as contemporary art and antique furniture. Decorator Frédéric Méchiche has that skill: this complex group is masterly in its clean composition.*

Below center *A primitive chair and a Shaker table, on which is a small collection of turned vessels, are made to connect with each other through the four pictures hung to define the outer limits of the group.*

Below far right *The tried and tested decorative device of arranging these objects in front of a mirror gives them a depth and resonance that would not be achieved if they were just ranged against a blank wall.*

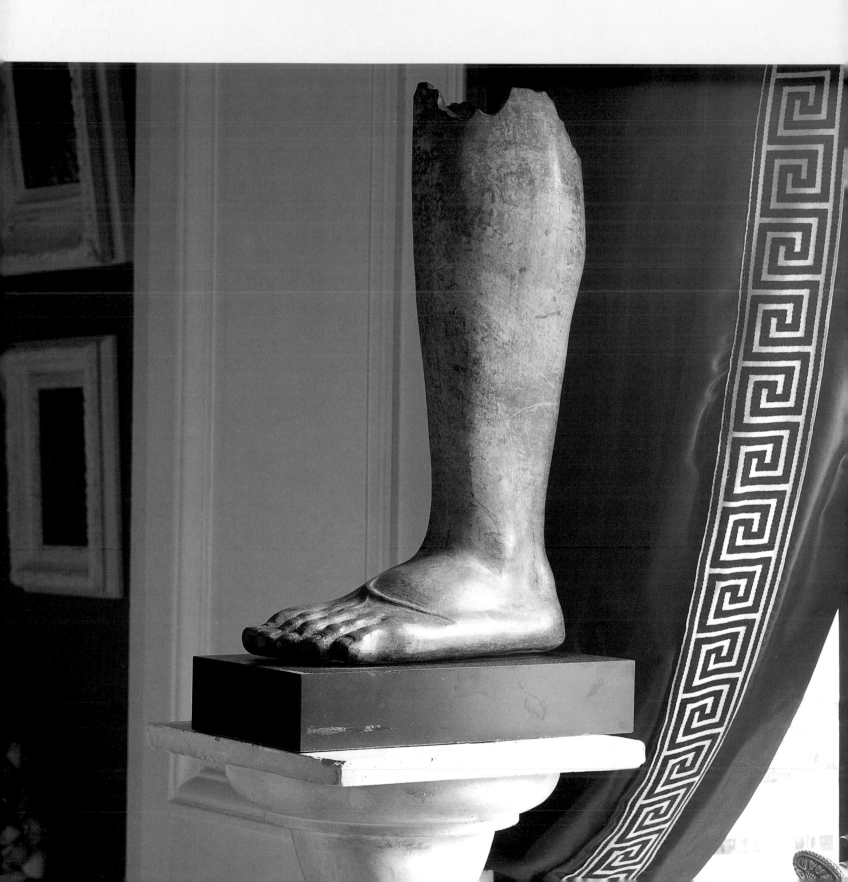

THE **ANTIQUARIANS**

The Antiquarian collector is the direct **descendant** of Renaissance and eighteenth-century devotees, and is lured by the **siren call** of the classical and the antique. The Antiquarian collects everything from fragments of ancient art to **shiny** neoclassical pieces.

Although one accepted definition of an antiquarian is someone who has a wide knowledge of early, often local, history, most people understand the word to mean one who collects the art and artifacts of ancient civilizations – in particular, those of ancient Greece and Rome. The Greeks – and to a slightly lesser degree, the Romans – created some of the most beautiful sculpture in marble and stone that the world has even seen, and it is only natural that lovers of art have always wanted to own a part, however small, of these artistic marvels.

For all the noise made during the eighteenth and early nineteenth centuries – particularly by the well-documented English Grand Tourists – about the newly found pleasures of classical art and architecture, the fact is that cultured Italians had long appreciated their classical past. They well knew both the aesthetic and the monetary worth of the art around them. Educated men of the Renaissance collected antiquities in quantity. Specific, famous statues were avidly pursued, and many a diarist of the time records the fabled collections of great Italian and French families. By the beginning of the seventeenth century, the collections of ancient sculpture amassed by such aristocratic and papal families as the Farnese, Medici, and Borghese were famous throughout Europe.

Many of the Renaissance Italian collections were partially broken up, and by the early 1600s, foreign connoisseurs were both traveling to Italy and commissioning local agents on their behalf who could look for and negotiate the purchase of existing and newly excavated antiquities. Among them was the 2nd Earl of Arundel, of the court of King Charles I, a scholarly and serious collector, who went to Italy on more than one occasion with advisors and agents; the high quality of the Arundel Marbles, as the 2nd Earl's acquisitions became known, made his collection famous throughout Europe. After the Earl's death, however, the collection was broken up and sold. When, a hundred years later, the diarist Mrs. Lybbe Powys saw part of it on display at the Schools in Oxford in 1759, the condition of many of the pieces had somewhat deteriorated. "We went to the Schools to take a survey of the statues, Lady Pomfret's present to the University, and which are styled an inestimable collection," she wrote. "I've no doubt by connoisseurs in ancient antiquities they may be thought so – their number is 135 – but I must own to have a taste so refin'd as to have no pleasure in the sight of so many dirty, frightful, maimed figures, some having unfortunately lost heads, others legs, arms, hands, or eyes. Being at a little distance from a Grecian Venus, the beauty of her face greatly struck me, but how was I forc'd to call my own judgement in question when on a nearer view I found it a new head stuck on by a late statuary on the dirty shoulders of a lady who seem'd to have no other merit but her having been form'd so many years ago."

EIGHTEENTH-CENTURY ZEAL

The collecting and acquisition of classical art reached its zenith during the eighteenth century, spurred on by the stream of new treasures being discovered at the excavations of the buried cities of Pompeii and Herculaneum. For many English nobles it was almost mandatory to have a collection of antique statuary. Families such as the Pembrokes acquired so much that Mrs. Lybbe Powys wrote that when she visited their family seat, Wilton House, in 1776 it looked more like a "statuary shop." The second Earl of Egremont amassed a fine collection of classical sculpture and built a gallery in his Sussex mansion, Petworth. At his house Ince Blundell, Henry Blundell displayed his classical remains in a gallery that was modeled on the Roman Pantheon. Huge prices were paid for

the eighteenth-century excavations of Pompeii and Herculaneum sparked a collecting mania for fragments of a classical past

choice pieces. In the 1780s, Sir William Hamilton, then British minister at Naples, paid a thousand pounds for a Roman antique cameo glass vase, which he later sold to the Duchess of Portland for nearly eighteen hundred guineas. The Portland vase still bears her name and can be seen today as a prize exhibit of the British Museum in London.

These impressive collections of classical art began to come onto the market – buyers being wealthy Italian families or equally wealthy, often royal, collectors from other countries. Even then, it was not easy to simply buy something and take it abroad; by the eighteenth century, excavations were regulated by law in the Papal states, and the export of works of art was subject to controls, under the aegis of a Commissioner of Antiquities. Most foreign collectors had to be content with bronze or plaster casts of the most significant sculptures that they saw on their travels.

In the nineteenth century, the tradition of collecting classical pieces was continued by wealthy men such as William Beckford and Thomas Hope (who bought much of William Hamilton's collection) and, a little later, by the 6th Duke of Devonshire. He collected both classical antiquities and neo-classical nineteenth-century marble sculpture, much of which can be seen at the family seat of Chatsworth in Derbyshire in England today. Across the Atlantic, the great collector J. Pierpont Morgan, whose spectacular buying spree was at its height between 1880 and 1905, naturally included antiquities in his all-encompassing range of collections. He moved swiftly through the great civilizations, buying the best of Greek and later the best of Egyptian art.

A collection of classical art and artifacts formed during this period gave its owner a strong sense of the romance of a lost, great civilization, as well as allowing him to enjoy the continuing excitement of the intermittent discovery of new, unknown treasures. Collecting classical art was also popular because it was widely understood by all men of education and taste that it not only represented the dignity and beauty of the human form idealized in sculpture, but also an intellectual concept of integrity and purity. These virtues were ones with which they were keen to be associated.

Left *Although so many pieces are shown together, this group is a visual treat, with the smaller pieces balanced by the larger. A collection of assorted architectural capitals, some of Coade stone, is used as a frame to the central composition.*

Right and far right *Busts have always been an important part of classical statuary. In Roman society, every successful citizen wished to be immortalized in marble, stone, or plaster, and the tradition persisted through the neoclassical period of the late eighteenth and early nineteenth centuries, right up to our own day. Peter Hone displays busts in vertical columns balanced on ornamental capitals to give them an added importance.*

AN OLD ROMANCE

This sense of the intellectual and artistic ideals that are encapsulated in classical art remains with us today, so it is not surprising that the collection of antiquities is still preeminent. Modern collectors, like those before them, appreciate the greatest art that the civilized world has perhaps ever known. It is hard not to be touched by a sense of the past, the idea of the history behind a piece of antique sculpture or a carved fragment of an architrave or capital. No matter how small, these fragments possess a mystery and, it would be fair to say, an always-present romance. And then there is the decorative aspect of antiquities. There is something about a piece of art carved from stone or marble that has a timeless appeal. From the start, the first antiquarian collectors understood the decorative power of the pieces they acquired. From Cardinal Mazarin's palace, decorated between 1645 and 1647, to the striking schemes of the eighteenth-century collector-builders and the later, more elaborate schemes of mid-nineteenth-century aficionados, these powerful pieces always took center stage. And it remains the same for today's collectors.

for anyone who thought that all these old pieces of
stone, marble, and plaster might look fusty or remote,
Peter Hone's apartment repays a second look

One of the associated joys of collecting
antiquities is that, unlike many other areas of
collecting, no one expects – in fact, it is a
bonus if it should be the case – an antiquity
to be perfect or complete. One antiquarian,
Peter Hone, actually finds perfection in a
fragment. He calls himself a collector of the
unwanted, unappreciated, orphaned; for him,
the pleasure of every piece comes from the
thought and attention to detail and material
shown by the original artist, as well the actual
skill involved in the crafting of each piece. It
is the quality of the total creation that
inspires him. His London apartment is a true
antiquarium – a space that would not look
out of place in an eighteenth-century interior
painting. Pieces of antique civilizations are

literally everywhere: every surface is covered
with fragments, some entire, of stone,
marble, and plaster.

Antique art is hung on walls, stacked and
lying on floors, sitting on tables; to move
through the space, a table top has to be
cleared, a bust moved to the side, a capital
shifted along. But this is not to say the
placing is haphazard – far from it. There is a
method and a discipline behind the
arrangement of the pieces. They are not
grouped together by type or age; instead, they
have been hung and placed in a rather
contemporary way, each positioned with a
fine regard for its essential shape and texture.
Each is used to make a small coherent group,
which repays careful study on its own and

Above left *Part of two different
collections, each with a shared
theme, are displayed by Peter
Hone here – classical reliefs and
neoclassical eighteenth-century
creamware. The two contrasting
groups are linked by the
universality of the classical
motifs they each employ.*

Above right *The so-called five
orders were an integral part
of classical architecture and
proscribed the different styles
and proportions suitable to
buildings. Here, the lower
column is Ionic and the upper
capital Corinthian.*

Above left *Classical motifs are many and varied, and are still used today in architectural decoration. Largely inspired by nature, they included several that are represented here – the acanthus leaf, the rosette and the anthemion or honeysuckle.*

Above right *A fitting bed for such a classical setting, Peter Hone's four-poster dressed in an old and beautiful chintz was originally made by John Fowler for Lady Anne Tree at Mereworth Castle. It is closely guarded by a Coade stone lion, once owned by Thomas Hope.*

which melds together into a cohesive whole. And for anyone who thought that all these old pieces of stone, marble, and plaster might look fusty or remote, the apartment repays a second look. Busts, heads, a foot or hand; urns and basins, statues large and small; architectural fragments, such as a carved stone capital or part of a pediment; bas-reliefs and plaques – all reveal so many shapes, designs, and materials. The range of design, pattern, and motif is surprisingly familiar, evidence of how much of the broad grammar of contemporary design originally stems from a classical repertoire. In addition to their decorative aspect, every piece of antiquity holds a historical fascination, because even though nearly every one is now a fragment, each might one day fit neatly into some architectural jigsaw, providing the final piece in some hitherto unknown research.

Peter Hone knows the recent provenance of every piece he owns: he documents where each piece was bought or found – whether from an auction room, country house, or yard sale, or even an abandoned house or dumpster. This knowledge inevitably leads to a further area of pleasure for the dedicated collector. An important part of any collector's life is the recognition and identification of a new treasure – particularly when the piece might be rare or of hidden value. This thrill of identification is very much a part of the antiquarian's makeup. Hone vividly recalls a sale, several years ago, in which a marble hippocamp – a mythical sea beast – was offered, complete with a cherub rider. "To me that piece was an original Roman piece, which had probably been restored in the eighteenth century," he remembers, although it was listed in the catalog as from the nineteenth century. He bought it, determined to find out more. Some time later, he noticed by chance a picture in a book of the famous sculpture collection at Wentworth Woodhouse, formed by the great collector Lord Rockingham in the eighteenth century. In the corner of the picture could be seen the unmistakable tail of a hippocamp –

Right *Michael Coorengel and Jean Pierre Calvagrac appreciate the intrinsic lines of the classical as well as its direct descendant, the neoclassical, and they like to combine the two in complex but comfortable room arrangements.*

Below left *In this true French enfilade, the long window wall in the apartment has been carefully styled in order to engage the eye, between each end of the apartment, with clever decorative details.*

Below right *A contrast of surprising color between the flowing rooms is important to Coorengel and Calvagrac; here, dramatic black-gray abuts a room with a color scheme of grape purple and brilliant red.*

Right *In contrast to the emphatic colors of the others, this hexagonal eating room has been painted in a neutral palette of light gray and white. Against this background, each pale piece stands out sharply.*

Below right *A contemporary and striking treatment for a collection of antique busts is designed in a narrow entrance hall. They seem to float on clear columns, with angled mirrors bonded behind each one, the better to appreciate their severe beauty.*

one that bore a very strong resemblance to his auction buy. Further research showed that Lord Rockingham had bought the piece in Italy while on his Grand Tour, and it was indeed Roman. From this, Peter Hone was able to trace its journey from sculpture hall to auction sale and verify that indeed his hippocamp and Lord Rockingham's were one and the same.

LIVING WITH THE PAST

The idea of the texture as well as the form of classical architectural fragments is often of particular interest to those who collect them. In the Paris apartment of Michael Coorengel and Jean Pierre Calvagrac, two of France's most successful young interior decorators, a collection of classical art is not kept in isolation, in a designated room, but is carefully placed throughout the apartment. Sometimes the antiquities contrast with other pieces; sometimes they are arranged in complementary fashion. Sometimes, as with the antique heads displayed on clear plastic plinths in a hall, they are presented in a way that is completely modern, yet timeless.

Coorengel and Calvagrac say that they "like to work with things that have a past, that speak for themselves, or with an object that we feel will have a past in the future – what you might call a classic to be." Like Peter Hone, they relish the fractured beauty of fragmented pieces. On a plinth stands a rather authoritative foot and leg; elsewhere, on a low column, a solitary head begs attention.

Coorengel and Calvagrac also like to combine the classical with its direct descendant, the neoclassical. They relate pieces, grouping them carefully so that you can see at first glance the lines of descent and common ground. "It's an instant story to do with antiquity; the neo-classical is an interpretation of what has gone before, and is balanced and harmonious with it," they explain. "As designers, we are sensitive to those balances." Throughout the apartment, they use color in a studied way, relating it closely to the arrangement of their

Above left *Seen from the neo-classical blue room, the bust on a plain white pediment at the far end of the apartment, of King William I of Holland, acts as a definitive decorative and architectural boundary.*

Left *The blue of the walls is inspired by the neoclassical mirror, found in an attic, and by the fluted Ionic columns. An exotic lamp and a French Empire daybed add unusual touches to the room.*

Right *Above the mantelpiece is a large classical medallion found at auction. To remove it from the sphere of the ordinary and give it depth – and wit – Coorengel and Calvagrac placed a small bisque group sculpture in front of it.*

collections. "Color is important in each room; it is part of both the collection and the overall design. For example, one room where many of our French Empire pieces are, is painted a particular shade of blue, while another room is colored in a dusky grape-purple. The function of color here is to blend everything together. When you collect things that are less 'good' just for the shape, then color helps to give them more intrinsic value."

The collections of antique dealers Laurent Dombrowicz and Franck Delmarcelle span a broader time base than that defined by the classical world. Their farmhouse in northern France is home to many different collections, but the overall feeling is of one vast homogeneous collection in which everything blends and melds together in an unforced harmony. Classical pieces – statues, urns and bas-reliefs – are combined with many other things – religious artifacts, Masonic art and neoclassical pieces. For example, a large collection of

Above *Laurent Dombrowicz and Franck Delmarcelle understand texture and tone: the beauty of these two models of hands – one clasped, one alone – comes in the contrast between rough and smooth and the carefully arranged composition.*

Left *It's not what you do, it's the way that you do it: not many would fill an urn with a bunch of assorted antlers and horns, but the arrangement adds the necessary height and dramatic contrast to this table display.*

Above right *A somber and dramatic composition of a nineteenth-century statue of the Virgin and a heavy urn is all the more telling when arranged against a background of rough beams, wooden walls, and restored tile floor.*

Wedgwood pieces, many based on the original eighteenth-century designs of Joseph Flaxman, himself inspired by the excavations at Pompeii, is part of the mix. Franck and Laurent are not the sort of collectors who search obsessively for a particular piece. "It is not a question of when and by whom – that would be boring," they suggest. "For us it is purely visual. Basically we buy what appeals to us visually, creating themes that we think will be appropriate for a room, like the shells in the bathroom. We very much identify with and relate to the eighteenth-century spirit, the interest in art and death, and the strong relationship between the mind and

man." And like eighteenth-century men, they are naturally drawn to the idea of classical art. Throughout the house, complete pieces or dramatic fragments are used to inform other pieces or to draw attention to a group. They also understand the importance of the varied textures and the patinas found in antiquities, Their collection is put to work to emphasize and throw into relief other pieces. A stone relief of a putto sits directly beneath a weathered wooden beam, resting on two large exotic shells. The contrast between textures could not be greater, and everything is pulled together by the sheer mass of the cherub. Elsewhere, a

larger-than-life classical statue is placed next to a fragile love seat covered in old toile de Jouy, the textural contrasts showing each element to best advantage.

It is interesting how very modern all the pieces shown here now appear. Perhaps that is part of the fascination of these ancient designs for the antiquarian that on so many different levels they hold our interest. Their appeal is wide, attracting the decorator, the sleuth, the conservator, and the designer. Whether they are used alone, or among other very different collections, antiquities always stand out, because every piece, no matter how small, is proof of the timelessness of art.

Right *The light, almost frail lines of the period settee covered in tapestry, and the grisaille painting behind it, in this hall emphasize the height and strength of the rather menacing helmet-clad plaster figure.*

THE **EXPLORERS**

The Explorer collector is a natural **discoverer**. While today this may not mean travel to **uncharted** polar or tropical regions, the Explorer's interest is still global – a fascination for objects **strange** and **different**, which illustrate the beauty of other lives.

Above *One of the eerily realistic collection of twenty-six armored samurai that Wade arranged in the Green Room to appear as the rendezvous of an army of warriors, each arrayed with weapons and battle-ready.*

Above left *In a corner of the Turquoise Hall at Snowshill Manor stands an ornate Chinese lacquered bureau with multiple drawers and broken, shaped pediment, made expressly – as so many were – for the export market in the mid-eighteenth century.*

Below left *In the Green Room, a gold and black lacquered Japanese Buddhist shrine, known as a Butsudan, has folding doors and screens, and is furnished with bronze and lacquered objects.*

Right *The Chinese cabinet that began Charles Paget Wade's collecting passion belonged to his grandmother. As a child, he would examine the contents on a Sunday – the only day it was allowed to be unlocked – and spin tall tales about their fabulous origins.*

century, there was also exploration from the Americas to Europe, and travelers started to form the collections from the New World. Richard Codman traveled to France during the period of chaos in the aftermath of the French Revolution, and was thus able to buy many pictures from newly impoverished aristocrats. His initial aim was to resell them in London or America, but many were kept by his brother, John, and later formed the basis of the Codman collection.

During the nineteenth century, the hitherto impenetrable world of the East became more accessible to Western travelers, and the arts of China and Japan became very fashionable. Many collectors were drawn to this new expression of artistic excellence by the explosion of color that was often typical of oriental style, seemingly so different from the measured tones of European objects. Charles Paget Wade was a consummate collector of artifacts from Persia and the Far East, in particular Japan, feeling that they demonstrated craftsmanship, color and design to the highest possible degree. Even today, the way that Wade displayed his Eastern artifacts

in Snowshill, his seventeenth-century Gloucestershire manor house, seems original and exciting. Enter the first-floor Green Room and you come face to face with a samurai shrine, apparently guarded by a fierce samurai warrior – a realistic, almost ghoulish model clad in a complete suit of armor. Wade injected a feeling of theatricality and drama into this room; it was lit, or rather hardly lit at all, so that the warriors were half-hidden in the gloom. The room became a stage set in which he could display his exotic treasures in the most dramatic way possible.

DIFFERENT WORLDS

Today's explorer-collectors still have much of the same sense of wonder. Some of them travel just as much as their predecessors, and others find their collections closer to home, but they are all still seduced by the strangeness, beauty, and exuberance of other cultures and other art forms. Parisians Françoise De Nobele and her husband combine their different enthusiasms brilliantly in their Paris apartment. While she collects all things natural and strange, her husband, Jean-Michel Smilenko, is a real explorer, fascinated by African art, particularly tribal masks. Every room has examples of this art, sitting comfortably with Françoise's eclectic collections of everything from ceramics to curiosities. Smilenko's passion began in the 1980s when he bought back his first mask from an African trip, and now he tracks them down wherever he can. In the apartment, the connection

Left *Françoise De Nobele and husband Jean-Michel Smilenko are true explorer-collectors. This corner of their Paris apartment combines African artefacts collected by Smilenko with curiosities from all over the world, about which De Nobele is passionate.*

Above right *Everywhere you look in this Parisian apartment, you see an object lesson in display. At first glance, the groups seem simple, but the unusual juxtapositions and combinations of elements are the product of careful thought.*

Above far right *Color and texture are the display links in operation in this small group. A red-lacquered African ornamental piece is slung across a dark-glazed ceramic pot; the color of the lacquer is echoed by the lamp base – an ornate figured urn.*

Right *African figures sit easily alongside objects that appear to be preserved bit players from the film* Jaws 3. *The encased mummified cat on one side of the arrangement is echoed by the small* memento-mori *picture on the wall on the other.*

Above left *The startlingly simple, barely adorned lines of African ornament mean that Peter Adler's pieces look as good displayed as elements of a decorative scheme as they do when worn as jewelry, as they were first intended.*

Below left *African artists and craftspeople use the natural bounty at their disposal to create objects of beauty. Organic materials such as shells, bones, horn, and tusks are all employed in the skilled making of ornamental objects and jewelry.*

Above right *Peter Adler has a fine and educated eye, as his collection of African artefacts shows. Here rare ceremonial African tribal hats made from dyed chicken feathers are displayed above a collection of woven pots.*

Above far right *Coorengel and Calvagrac combine East with West with a sophisticated eye. A heavy French desk and an ornate gilded frame have both been painted white and are displayed with a Chinese-inspired, tasseled chandelier from the 1950s.*

Below right *Belgian decorator Agnès Emery collects batik cloth, examples of an ancient Eastern design technique that uses wax to protect areas during dyeing. She combines different cloths with other pieces of brocade and damask, and transforms them into striking costumes for herself.*

Below far right *Kente cloths – the generic name for traditional African strips of textile woven from cotton or silk and then sewn together – are dazzling in their diversity of pattern and range of color and design.*

for explorers, combing the world for one discovery often leads on to another – to a fresh search and to the start of a new collection

between the naturalist's and the explorer's worlds can be clearly seen in arrangements that combine to a seamless degree. Perhaps it is because much of African art has a directness that works well with the natural; or it may be the way in which the shapes work together. For example, in one room a mask is balanced upon a shell; and a large picture of tribal life acts as a backdrop for a grouping of fossils and stone-carved figures. Skulls and painted masks nestle against each other in this collection, and there is a natural fluidity between them all.

Laurent Dombrowicz and Franck Delmarcelle also explore, but closer to home. They are mental as well as physical explorers, finding that, like the good cliché says, travel for a collector broadens the mind. "Often the discovery of one thing leads to a new search and discovery of others," they explain. "This happened with the glazed pots above the fireplace in the kitchen. We were traveling in Hungary when we saw a pot, liked it, and bought it, not knowing anything about it. Then we saw another, then a third, and suddenly we had a group, a

collection. With this type of object, one is not interesting; it only makes sense if you have several. It is the visual accumulation that is fascinating."

Many objects collected by explorers serve to remind them, and those who see the objects, of the ways of different worlds. For example, when you see the many paper dress patterns brought back by Diane de Clercq from Kenya, you can visualize the roadside tailor at his sewing machine, making a dress to be ready in an hour. Peter Adler knows this, since he has long collected tribal art. "The collecting began because I was touring America, and I became fascinated by Native American culture; later, I became aware of Afro-Oceanic art. I knew that I should learn as I went, which is one of the wonderful things about collecting tribal art – or collecting anything for that matter." His apartment is stuffed with tribal pieces – headpieces, necklaces, and bracelets made from teeth, bone, and horn, containers, carved figures, masks, traditional woven textiles – all put together in a way that is not entirely haphazard, but that relies on a jewel-box effect.

CULTURAL INSPIRATION

Hubert Zandberg also collects ethnic art – partly for its beauty and partly for the memories his pieces hold. Brought up in South Africa, his tiny apartment in London is filled with ethnic pieces, in particular a collection of beautiful, extravagantly decorated headdresses, which have for him a resonance that is perhaps lacking for some Westerners. "To me, a headdress isn't just an object, it gives you back something. Many of these pieces are my youth, as well as my memories." We may not be able to share Hubert Zandberg's memories, but we can certainly appreciate the beauty and style of the headdresses. These are made even stronger by the sophisticated way in which Zandberg displays them. Throughout the apartment, they are used as decorative elements, worked in with other disparate objects to make a harmonious whole. One is used for its color tones, another for its contrasting shape. Adorned with cowry shells and seeds, displayed on small hat stands, each stands alone and appears very contemporary. In one room there is a strong arrangement in which headdresses are combined with different objects all relatively similar in shape – a hat mold, a sphere and, rather wittily, an angled lamp whose stem echoes the stands of the hats. In another, color is the key: the hot colors of headpieces and tribal objects are combined in an eye-stopping group. Zandberg knows that there are limits to what you can do: "It is important to be immediate when you arrange collections, and also to know when to stop," he advises. "It doesn't always have to be perfect; it is second nature to me to place things in a certain way, although others might call that obsessive."

Left *Although combined with other natural objects, Africa dominates this corner of decorator Hubert Zandberg's London apartment. The color scheme – tawny gold and deep brown – is that of the veldt, and draws all the elements in the room together.*

Above right *Zandberg's gift is of displaying beautiful but difficult objects, such as these tribal hats, as pieces of contemporary art. Each shape, including the angled lamp, is seen as a sculptural piece in its own right.*

Below right *A striking display in the tiny hall includes a ceremonial tribal chicken-feather hat from Africa as the centerpiece of a vertical group that uses color and symmetry to make its impact.*

"the Buddhas transformed from being objects to having a spiritual quality – they took on a life and had connections"

Vicente Wolf is not obsessive, but he certainly knows what he is doing when arranging an interior. He goes abroad a lot, buying objects to use and sell in his interior design business, and at heart he is a true explorer. "I would say that seventy-five per cent of my collection has come through travel and through having been exposed to things that were out of the norm for me," he says. "The uniqueness and curiosity of the things that I have seen just stirred me and made me want to collect them. It is as if they touched a chord or pressed a button in the core of my soul. The Buddhas, for example, I first bought to sell to clients in America, but then they took on a life of their own. Suddenly, they transformed from being objects to having a spiritual quality – they took on a life and had connections."

He goes on to explain the origins of his passion. "My education came from museums, and I still go there to learn to appreciate different things. My collection of pipes is another based on my travels. It started when I went to Laos; I found a couple of pipes there and then my eyes were opened. I think it

is because they have been smoked that they are so important to me; they are like little jewels and they have a history. I know where I bought each one." Whenever Wolf travels, he allows himself a treat; it may be art, and in the Far East it may well be another Buddha. He does try not to become too attached to his treasures. "We only have them for a time, these objects. They are not just for us; others have owned them in the past and hopefully will have them in the future. It has given me a freedom to let them go when necessary." And perhaps that is something which, with their pan-vision, all explorers know.

Above far left *When decorator Vicente Wolf is in charge, nothing is left to chance. A table group of African masks is carefully arranged to make a pleasing, rounded display, with height being added by the gilded candle stand.*

Left *The eternal, solitary serenity of the Buddha is emphasized here by the careful spacing of this peaceful pair, which is anchored by a subtle monochrome background.*

Above *Every true explorer-collector knows the background of every item in his collection, and each of these pipes, many of them bought by Vicente Wolf in Laos, has a story behind it.*

THE **INHERITORS**

The Inheritor collector is a person with a past; it may be an **actual past** represented by an existing, inherited collection, or it might simply be a **keen sense** of the past. In either case, the Inheritor is committed to collecting in the manner of his forebears, maintaining a **tradition**.

Although most people associate inheritance with a financial settlement, it can, in fact, adopt many different forms. For a collector, a financial inheritance could provide the wherewithal for the development from scratch of a new collection. On the other hand, the inheritance could itself consist of an entire existing collection – large or small, of monetary or purely sentimental value. Or, thinking laterally, an inheritance could be genetic – the passing down through the generations of the taste with which to build up a collection of the first order, and the inclination to do so.

The excessive and romantic Englishman William Beckford, for example, collected throughout the late eighteenth and the early nineteenth centuries. He possessed not only leisure time and education, but also, from 1770, an inheritance of the enormous Beckford fortune, derived from West Indian sugar, and the ownership of the substantial Fonthill House in Wiltshire in southern England. Beckford was a collector on a grand scale, whose taste and vision were acknowledged in his own time as superb – although William Hazlitt dismissed him as "an enthusiastic collector of expensive trifles." His interest was wide-ranging and he constantly reinvented his collections, buying and selling assiduously, until he lost his money when the sugar market collapsed.

As a result of his loss, his marvellous collections were broken up and sold. He staged a gigantic and spectacular sale of his possessions at Fonthill House in 1822. A contemporary report in *The Times* of London recorded: "accommodation was provided in a pavilion in the park, beds being charged 3/6 single, 5/- double..." and that "the beds through the country are literally doing double duty; people who come in from a distance during the night must wait to go to bed until others get up in the morning. Not a farmhouse, however humble, not a cottage near Fonthill but gives shelter to fashion, to beauty and rank; ostrich plumes, which by their very waving, we can trace back to Piccadilly, are seen nodding at a casement window over a depopulated poultry yard." Beckford's sale was clearly a glamorous event, one not to be missed.

Above right *Charles Paget Wade inherited from his father the money to buy Snowshill and to fill it with his collections from all over the world. This room, Dragon, contains a collection of the coats of arms of previous owners, as well as suits of armor and paintings.*

Below right *In the Codman House in Massachusetts, every room holds objects that were passed down from one generation to the next. In the dining room, a cabinet is filled with nineteenth-century china, including a set bearing the Codman monogram.*

THE INHERITANCE OF A NATION

In one sense we are all inheritors, because most of the great public collections across the world were originally formed through the drive and commitment of a single person or family. Originally, there were no large public museums – a gentleman's collection would be displayed in his house or, if large enough, in a building expressly constructed for the purpose. Richard, 3rd Earl of Burlington, went perhaps slightly farther than his contemporaries, building an entire small mansion outside London, Chiswick House, which was based on a design by Andrea Palladio and constructed for the

sole purpose of housing his collection. Other collectors commissioned rather grand purpose-built rooms and galleries from the leading architects of the day – Robert Adam built a sculpture gallery for William Weddell at Newby Hall in Yorkshire, for example. These collections could usually be viewed on application to the house; it was not necessary to know the owner socially. A member of the household staff, able to point out the works of particular interest, usually conducted the tour, and in some areas there were specific days reserved for the gentry and others on which "ordinary" members of the general public could come. Horace Walpole, who kept his many and varied collections in his "little play-thing house," Strawberry Hill at Twickenham, found himself and his collections so famous that he issued tickets for the general public to come and admire both the architecture of the house and his objects. The viewing season at Strawberry Hill lasted from May to September, and over the years at least 10,000 interested travelers sampled its delights, which ranged from ephemera to important works of art.

Over time, these private collections became available to a wider audience. One of the earliest public collections was that of Elias Ashmole, born in 1617, whose Ashmolean Museum in

Above center *It is rare to see such a perfect cabinet of curiosities, with nature as its theme. Inherited from a seventeenth- and eighteenth-century idea, it celebrates nature's beauty, from the butterfly collages to the cabinet itself, decorated with fern specimens.*

Above right *Taste is a quality that is not always inherited, although in Emma Hawkins' case it evidently has been. In her Edinburgh house, a handsome early nineteenth-century cupboard is the background for a simple collection of stone pestles and mortars.*

Far left *The story of the Codman House today is the story of Ogden Codman Jr.'s, re-styling of it in the early 1900s. Trained as an architect and decorator, he took a great interest in the interior, simplifying its heavy and overbearing Victorian taste.*

Left *A small nineteenth-century group in Mrs Codman Sr.'s, bedroom, including two thermometers – one set into an Egyptian obelisk, the other into a classical column – reflects the passions of the time.*

Above right *In the drawing room, many paintings are on show, including a portrait of Richard Codman by John Singleton Copley, probably painted in England in 1794 before Codman journeyed to Paris to buy the first of the paintings to enter the family collection.*

Above far right *In the bedroom of Ogden Codman's sister Alice, he restored the original paneling and painted the room in a light color. The original medallion toile fabric has faded to different degrees, giving a charming, rather subtle effect.*

Below right *An imposing inlaid cabinet in the drawing room holds some of the varied ceramic collection. The cabinet was brought back to Massachusetts by Ogden Codman Sr., when the family returned from their self-imposed exile in France during the 1880s.*

an inheritance may be of an entire collection, but it may also be genetic – the passing on down the generations of a taste and enthusiasm for collecting

Oxford was founded in 1683. It displayed the fruits of his own collecting, as well as the ethnological collections he was bequeathed on the death in 1662 of his friend, the gardener and botanist John Tradescant the Younger. Tradescant had had a small museum of curiosities at Lambeth in London, nicknamed the Ark, with such exhibits as, according to John Evelyn in 1657, "Ancient Roman, Indian and other nations' armour, shields and weapons; some habits of curiously coloured and wrought feathers, one from the phoenix wing, as tradition goes."

There are probably far more people at the opposite end of the inheritance spectrum – those who inherit little or nothing. To be left comparatively little can, perversely, be a blessing to the true collector, for those who inherit great possessions often feel that they are tied to their stewardships. Rather than collectors, they are custodians and caretakers for the next generation. Certainly, many fine collections that were not dispersed at the death of the owner were built up in Europe and later in America over the eighteenth and nineteenth centuries. Richard Rush, American Ambassador to the Court of St. James between 1817 and 1825, wrote in his memoirs that "England contained more paintings than any other country, not in public depositories, for there were none worth speaking of, but in private houses; the rich bought up the best upon the continent, wherever to be had." This observation demonstrates the fact that in order to inherit a collection, it first has to be built by someone. It is not that inheritors as a group never sell or lose pieces, but on the whole, they have a feeling for the possessions that represent a family. Many inheritors consciously try to rebuy the artifacts, pictures, and furniture that once belonged to their families. The beneficiaries of these inheritances could find themselves dominated by the idea of "the collection." Horace Walpole regretted, for the whole of his long life, that the collection of paintings at

Houghton Hall in Norfolk built up by his father, Sir Robert Walpole, had been sold by his cousin, who inherited the estate. Most went to Catherine the Great of Russia, one of the world's great collecting predators.

ARRANGING HISTORY

All over the world, there are families who still live with the collections built up by their forebears. The Codman family of Massachusetts are a case in point. They inherited what is today known as the Codman House in Lincoln, Massachusetts at the end of the eighteenth century, but a few years later it was sold. In 1862, Ogden Codman Sr., grandson of the first owner, bought it back. Although, as a result of the family falling on relatively hard times, it was leased out for long periods, by 1880 the family was re-ensconced. The house was filled with fine pieces of furniture, portraits, objects, and memorabilia, much inherited from earlier generations, including a collection of paintings that had been largely acquired during the 1790s by Richard Codman in confused, revolutionary France. After the death of Ogden Senior and his

Left *Originally known as the Billiard Room, complete with what Ogden Codman Jr., called in 1897 "that dreadful billiard table," the library is today the way he redecorated it at the end of the nineteenth century.*

Right *Through the door from the hall – still with a ready-to-use umbrella stand – can be seen the library, with one of the chairs made in the late eighteenth century for the Senate Chamber of the then new State House in Boston.*

Below *In the paneled parlor stands a lacquered Chinese cabinet, passed down through the family, which was made in the late eighteenth century specifically for export to the new United States.*

wife in the 1920s, their five children inherited the house and spent much of their time consolidating the family possessions, buying pieces back from other branches and arranging them all in the Codman house. These last descendants of the Codman family all died childless, the last surviving child, Dorothy, in 1968. All the many layers and generations' worth of Codman possessions remained intact and can be seen *in situ* today, courtesy of the Society for the Protection of New England Antiquities (SPNEA), which administrates and opens the house.

There are also other sorts of collecting inheritances, such as the receipt of one solitary object. This might be a piece that can open the eyes and the mind of the inheritor and lead on to other collecting interests. Charles Paget Wade, twentieth-century designer and owner of Snowshill in Gloucestershire, was one such, inheriting an ornate, eighteenth-century, lacquered Chinese cabinet from his grandmother. It was a true cabinet of curiosities, with drawers and compartments, and as a child he had been allowed to open and explore its contents –

Above left *The black Formica table in the Gropius's dressing room runs the length of a ceiling-high glass partition dividing off the bedroom.*

Above right *In the living room, a plywood laminate daybed designed in 1925 for the Isokon firm in England is covered with a sheepskin. It was shipped to the United States with the rest of Walter and Ise Gropius's furniture after they were forced to leave Germany in the 1930s.*

Center left *In the entrance hall leading into the study, the walls are covered with vertical clapboards, painted white; their narrow vertical shadows relieve the blandness.*

Center right *The bathroom is as it was designed in 1937, with the original equipment. Surprisingly contemporary, the mirror conceals one of the earliest set-in bathroom cabinets. Not seen here are shiny black rubber floor tiles. As throughout the house, the only accent color is red.*

Below left *As might be expected, even the dishes were of concern to Walter and Ise Gropius, although they were uninterested in the practical side of cooking, and these examples are plastic. The table was designed by Marcel Breuer in 1925 and made at the Bauhaus.*

Below right *The desk made for and used by both Walter and Ise Gropius was designed in 1925 by Marcel Breuer to Gropius's specifications for the Director's House in Dessau; the chairs were designed by Saarinen.*

the Gropius House encapsulates the culture of twentieth-century Europe – and the belief of its designer owners in a functional aesthetic

Above *The north façade of the Gropius house was revolutionary at the time, with its flat roof, ribbon windows, and plate-glass and glass blocks. The spiral staircase was installed so that their then twelve-year-old daughter could get to her room in privacy – although it was overlooked by the study.*

Right *The study was divided from the dining area by a glass brick wall that shuts off noise but allows the room to be part of the general space. The ribbon window runs the length of the desk and gives essential northern light.*

Far right *The living room, the largest part of the open-plan ground floor, has the same width as the study and dining room combined. It appears as a coherent space with the dining room, from which it can be divided by a curtain.*

toys and treasures from his grandmother's own childhood, keepsakes that stirred his own imagination. From that moment, he began to collect, and the fever not only never left him, but also increased in leaps and bounds, so that by the time he bought Snowshill in 1919, he had enough objects to fill several of its many rooms.

CULTURAL HERITAGE

The collections and their arrangement at Snowshill were a collection of the accouterments of living. On the other hand, the collections and house of Walter and Ise Gropius, which first their daughter and now the American people have inherited, are a

Emma Hawkins has inherited an inspired taste – for the beauty that is to be found in her antiques and her treasures from the natural world

reflection of the culture of twentieth-century Europe – in particular, of the Bauhaus in Dessau, of which Walter Gropius was founder and director. This was also the inheritance of a dream and a belief – in this case, the unshakeable belief of both Walter and Ise Gropius in their art and their ideals. Forced to leave Germany in 1937, they arrived in the U.S. via London. Walter was offered the job of chairman of the Architectural Department of Harvard's Graduate School of Design, and also, by a local philanthropist, a plot of land in Lincoln, Massachusetts. There he designed and built a house that espoused the ideals of the Bauhaus and provided a suitable setting for the couple's collection of furniture and

artifacts, which they were able to have sent on from Berlin. The house was more than just a decorative setting; certain areas were specifically designed to accommodate particular pieces of furniture. For example, the dimensions of the study were formulated to hold the large double desk that had been designed for them in 1925 by the Bauhaus carpentry shop.

What the Gropiuses had around them in their new American life was – perhaps unconsciously – a collection of the best of the functional aesthetic of the Bauhaus, evident, for example, in furniture designed by Marcel Breuer and Walter Gropius. They also owned pieces made by like-minded designers, including Japanese furniture and pictures, and

Above left *In Emma Hawkins'
Edinburgh kitchen, members of
her vast stuffed aviary, as well
as the odd piscine specimen, sit
expectantly, as if waiting for
food to be prepared and set out
on the kitchen table below.*

Above center *Adding height to
the chimney-piece arrangement,
a pair of jagged sawfish bills
flank a mirror, clock, and two
giant clamshells. To the right,
an antique display cabinet holds
a collection of finely turned
wooden treen.*

Above right *In the center of
the Hawkins drawing room,
a sturdy sideboard is home to
varied natural collections; on
top is a carefully positioned
group of Victorian domed-glass
cases, each one containing an
object that demands attention.*

works of art by such luminaries as Paul Klee, Wassily
Kandinsky, and Henry Moore, and by Bauhaus artists such as
Josef Albers, László Moholy-Nagy, and Herbert Bayer.

An inheritance can be of ideals, taste, or a view of life.
Antique dealer Emma Hawkins has inherited commitment and
inspired taste from her father John, president of the Australian
Antique Dealers' Association. He is a man of vision, noticing
first the potential of the Regency house in Edinburgh where
she displays her eclectic collections; and he helped her stock
her first antique shop in London. Although she maintains she
would sell any part of her several collections, it is evident
from the care she takes with their display, and the warmth
with which she discusses some of the stranger pieces, that she
has the true instincts of a collector – curiosity and affection
for her charges. She sees a true beauty in her ever-changing
collection of taxidermy, assorted coral, shells, feathers, and
pelts, and is more than happy to share her pleasure.

The inheritance of collecting taste can also be seen in the young daughter of designer Reed Krakoff; in her room, there is burgeoning evidence. On her bedroom walls are three sketches by designer Bill Blass, cheerful in their pinks and reds that blend with pink and purple suede stools, part of the furniture line of the Coach company. Over her desk is a large photograph of Barbie by Sheila Metzner, and on the mantelpiece a selection of fashion sketches and a drawing by Jean Cocteau. This is a careful nurturing of a truly artistic inheritance. And perhaps Diane de Clercq sums up instinctive collecting skills when she says that "the idea of collecting is almost ingrained in me; my great grandfather collected boats, large boats, and all my family collect in their different ways, without discussing it or making much of it. I myself don't collect as a defined occupation: I just buy things – the things I like to have around me and those which connect to my life."

Above left *Inherited taste is an interesting concept. This is obviously a young girl's room – light, bright and with colorful touches – but it does show an underlying discipline in the way that the Bill Blass sketches are grouped, and in the off-center placing of the suede stools.*

Left *At the other end of the room, two collections meet – one of fashion illustration in all its forms, the other of Reed Krakoff's collection of unusual and interesting furniture. In this grown-up child's room, the dolls are on the walls, not strewn on the floor.*

Right *An exemplary demonstration of the art of displaying a collection is seen in pictures ranged one behind the other in interesting layers and with thematic associations – such as the rose corsage illustrated in the photograph and the rose-scattered hat in the large drawing.*

THE **PERFECTIONISTS**

The Perfectionist collector will only consider acquiring the **most perfect** example of its kind – depending, of course, on the definition of perfect. It may be **rarity** or **flawless** condition or **great beauty**. But whatever the definition, the Perfectionist will accept nothing less.

Left *A row of "Flivvers," designs in the famous and very collectable Buddy L line of model pressed-steel cars collected by Jerry and Susan Lauren. Produced during the 1920s and 30s, they were advertised as "sturdy, all-steel, true-to-form reproductions."*

Right *Among the Buddy L line were dump trucks, lumber trucks, ice trucks, and coal trucks with chutes. The Laurens have many of the models, all in as perfect condition as possible. Displayed in this way, their charms are instantly evident.*

they found an old warehouse full of Buddy L American toy trucks in perfect condition – "That," sighs Jerry Lauren, "was the Holy Grail!"

For many collectors, perfection is the paramount, the ultimate, indeed, the only consideration when deciding whether or not to invest in a new acquisition. Whatever the size, whatever the type, an object or artifact must be perfect – and usually also be the best in its own field.

Interestingly, the definition of perfection is not one that is universally agreed or documented. Like beauty, perfection is to a large extent in the eye of the beholder; and where a collector is concerned, the beholder's eye is very personal. Of course, the words "flawless" and "faultless" do usually and immediately spring to mind, and for many, these are the only adjectives that count. But for some, perfection is found in something far from flawless, maybe in something positively distressed. Old teddy bears are

examples; most of them, well-loved and usually well-used, are in a far from perfect physical state, yet the rarity of particular designs renders them perfect to collectors of the genre. For others, a definition of perfection could be the moment of finding the final, elusive piece of a known set, or one that was hitherto unknown and undocumented. All such definitions have their adherents, and all are equally valid.

ONLY THE BEST

Some collectors follow several different perfect paths. Jerry and Susan Lauren, who live in a white-walled, sunlit apartment in Manhattan, are collectors of the first order. For them, first of all, the search is a hunt, an adventure to find the best examples of their particular specialities. They are dogged

in their pursuit of objects, visiting auctions, dealers, and fairs with a single-minded (or, rather, double-minded) concentration that all the best collectors have in common. As a general rule, they insist on perfection in the object itself, but its state is not necessarily defined by the flawlessness of its condition. If something is rare, perfection has another meaning: "We don't want to buy something with a crack in it if we can avoid it, and for us restoration or 'improvement' does not work. It is a question of purity, and also one of authenticity; for us, that characterizes the art of collecting."

The Laurens therefore collect both the pristine and the well-worn. A marvelous collection of American arts and crafts, dating mainly from the late nineteenth and early twentieth centuries, falls into the second category. They

refuse to call their specialty "folk art", which they consider a whimsical term that demeans the nature of the objects. Nor do they particularly care for the word "collection", which they feel alludes to the amassing of objects in bulk. Naturally, many of the pieces in this particular collection are very far from mint in condition. Their weathervanes were once hard-working outdoor objects with a distinct purpose in life; as a result, they are worn, the color chipped, the metal tarnished and in places a little rusty. Weathervanes in new and shiny mode would simply not have the same resonance or authenticity as these examples; the patina of time gives these simple forms a new, desirable, and deep beauty, one that is enhanced by the way in which they are displayed throughout the apartment. They stand like the sculptures they really are. Silhouetted in front of a window with the Manhattan skyline behind them, in stark relief against a white wall or reflected in front of a mirror, they need no aesthetic explanation. Some are raised high on contemporary plinths, and others are displayed with an authenticity that refers to their first life, when they would have been perched on a barn roof or farmhouse chimney.

Above left *Throughout Jerry and Susan Lauren's apartment in Manhattan, their collections are treated with the dignity that is accorded to pieces of sculpture. In the living room, part of their American weathervane collection is displayed as if it were in an art gallery.*

Above right *This very rare weathervane, in the form of a fast-paced horse and its rider, is placed in front of a tall window so that the pair almost seem to be trotting through the streets of the busy city outside.*

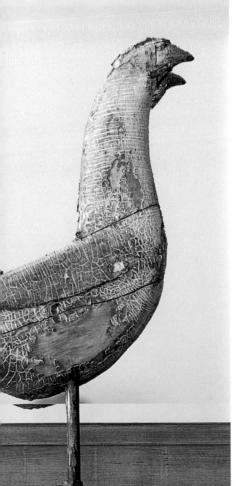

Above right *Silhouetted on a plinth, this purposeful nineteenth-century dog is reflected in the mirror and brought into juxtaposition with the weathervane of an Indian figure on the opposite wall and, in the corner, a rare double horse-head hitching post.*

Left *A late nineteenth-century rooster – a common subject for weathervanes – is made from wood, with a combed neck, and stands in front of a mirror. Its beauty lies in its condition – proof of its once hard-working outdoor life.*

In contrast to such rural pieces, in the other area of specialized interest for Jerry and Susan Lauren, condition is everything and the pristine definition of perfection comes into play. They have an outstanding collection of the American toy cars and trucks produced under the Buddy L label in the early 1920s. Highly sought-after today, they are seen by collectors not only as toys, but also as artifacts. The earliest model, a sit-on toy car known as "The Red Baby", was originally made by F. A. Lundhal for his son Buddy out of pressed steel scraps from the factory where he worked. Soon every child on the block wanted one, and the Buddy L company was in business. Dump trucks, fire engines, railroad cars, ice cars, and coal trucks complete with chutes became part of the line, each a faithful copy of its larger counterpart and advertised as a "sturdy, all-steel, true-to–form reproduction". Finding examples of Buddy L designs, particularly The Red Baby, in good condition is never easy. Imagine, then, Jerry and Susan's feelings when they discovered an old warehouse filled with new trucks, many still in their boxes, and prototypes of other designs, some half painted, and with the untreated steel showing through! "That," sighs Jerry, "was the Holy Grail."

Below *A fine group of 1870s Minton porcelain in the Japanese taste, some designed by Christopher Dresser, is displayed in a cabinet designed by Charles Bevan and made by Lamb of Manchester (England).*

Right *Perfectionists like themes – such as "The Englishman Abroad," featuring watercolors and drawings of European views, including one of Florence by John Bunney of 1863/4.*

Far right *The drawing room is a Victorian treasure house. On the mantelpiece is a fine pair of 1872 Royal Worcester vases, and the paintings include a study for William Holman Hunt's The Light of the World.*

THE ROAD TO PERFECTION

Although all perfectionists seek excellence of one sort or another, they do not always begin their collecting careers with such aspirations. Paul Dawson and Harold Galloway, who collect the best of Victorian art and crafts, began simply by buying what they could afford. They liked what they bought – of course they did – but it was not until they made the acquaintance of more serious collectors that they began to learn more, to look closely at pieces, and to become generally more selective. Most collectors find that the more knowledge they possess, the more that they appreciate a genre and start to seek out the best that it has to offer. Paul Dawson explains that "when we began collecting, we had friends who were fond of what they called Victoriana, so we went for "amusing

things" – wool pictures, novelty glass, knickknacks." They bought at all the London auction houses and in street markets, with their taste developing all the while, until about ten years later they realized that they had lost their early penchant for Victoriana. During the 1960s, they began collecting in a more serious vein, advised by knowledgeable and scholarly collector friends, like Charles and Lavinia Handley-Read, who opened their eyes to the fine furniture and art of the period.

Glass, ceramics, paintings, watercolors – all came under Dawson and Galloway's exacting scrutiny. As they learned more, they became more involved with people who knew about their specialized areas, and so they developed their knowledge still further. Perfectionists usually read widely in their field and often join relevant societies or clubs – the Victorian Society, in the case of Dawson and Galloway – where they meet other like-minded enthusiasts. Greater knowledge about a subject leads to greater collecting excitements when a chance discovery is identified and acquired before anyone else figures out what it is. The expert pair discovered a painting by Ford Madox Brown that was wrongly attributed at auction in Sussex, for example, and a table designed by E.W. Godwin that sat unrecognized in another English saleroom until they spotted its qualities.

In their Regency house of many rooms – each playing host to a facet of their Victorian passion – there is a sense, even

Left *The nineteenth century was famous for its grotesque and other strangely crafted stoneware. These pieces of Doulton salt-glazed pottery were decorated by Frank Butler, who was a highly talented and successful designer, despite being deaf and mute from birth.*

Below *"Like being inside a hat box," says the owner fondly of this room devoted to the Aesthetic Movement and to those crafts so beloved of Victorian ladies, such as the papier-mâché face screens, employed to protect their faces from the heat of the fire.*

Above right *A fine cabinet, attributed to Christopher Dresser, holds a collection of delicate straw opaline, blue Whitefriars glass of the late nineteenth century, inspired by the blown glass of the Venetians, who were, according to the critic John Ruskin, the true artists of glass.*

Far right *A room devoted to the Arts and Crafts movement contains the work of French studio potters Ernest Chaplet, August Delaherche, and Lévy d'Hurmer for Clément Massier. Above is a platter made by Eleonore Escallier for Theodore Deck. The Moorish table and copper mirror are by Liberty.*

Center right *So profuse are the collections that they spill into the kitchen, where on a distinctive hutch by Bruce Talbot are fine nineteenth-century relief-molded pitchers, flanking a Silicon Ware cheese-dish by Doulton.*

Below right *In this room, the central electrolier was designed by W.A.S. Benson, a close associate of William Morris. The bronzes, Perseus holding the head of Medusa by Pomeroy and The Sluggard by Lord Leighton, flank a clock of three faces, telling day and month, weather and moon, and time.*

without specialized knowledge, that displayed in front of you is the absolute best of nineteenth-century decorative and artistic life. In every room and on every surface, the proof is to be found: ceramics that range from pitchers and plates to tiles and platters; and nineteenth-century (and a smattering of twentieth-century) glass. There is an eclectic collection of furniture – much of it rare and beautiful, some eccentric and interesting – and oil paintings, watercolors, and drawings. There is also a wide range of those objects that are, and always have been, beloved of the really passionate collector: curiosities – natural and artificial, some fascinating, others beautiful, and some about which one can say nothing more than, "how very curious."

They know the provenance and history behind each piece and how and, more importantly, why it came into their possession. In each room, you are gently instructed in the history of art and design while you admire the collection and

hear a new story. Learning worn lightly is a great and rare art, and one ably demonstrated by these perfectionists.

If all other things are equal, Dawson and Galloway like to buy pieces that are flawless and to bring together objects that have a visual or contextual connection, which sometimes means thinking laterally. They cite the ceramics designed by the Pre-Raphaelite artist William de Morgan, examples of which are displayed in their bathroom, as a case in point. "From the very beginning, we convinced ourselves that we were too late to form a collection of de Morgan lusterwares, because his work was too well known and consequently too expensive, but we did like it very much. So, of course, we bought pieces when we saw them, telling ourselves that it was ridiculous to pay so much. But the happy fact is that his work has become more valuable, so by selling as well as buying we have been able to keep up with the market – in fact, our latest piece was bought only last week."

same emotion. This man has a place in almost every possible category of collector. He is a passionate, an explorer, and an enthusiast, but above all he is a perfectionist, both in what he collects and in the way in which he shows it to best effect in his huge, white-walled space. Wolf feels that when you enter someone's home, you step into a very particular environment – the place where the owner's personality is presented for approval or dissection. To this end, everything in the apartment – particularly those objects which have been collected for pleasure – is shown to perfect advantage.

Every detail of Wolf's collection is important. "Even if what I collect are pieces that no one else is interested in, that's still very important in its way," he explains. And it shows. Against one wall is a row of chairs, a deceptively simple device, but each chair is different and each interacts with its neighbor. Perfection for Wolf is also a question of immediacy: "Wonderful collections have never been premeditated, but have always just evolved. If you go for a set thing, it loses its spontaneity. Any collection must be personal and that must come from the fact that it is of overwhelming interest to the collector." He even defines how many pieces are required, deeming that you should "never have less than three of anything; three is a collection – two is just stuff."

The idea of perfection has many different faces and interpretations, and can come in many guises; and those who espouse it have very different tastes and characteristics. Yet it is interesting that the quality itself – however nebulous – is instantly recognized, even by those who would not ever identify themselves as being of the perfect persuasion. Those collectors who know themselves to be perfectionists will never accept that which they feel to be second rate, or the not quite right. It is this rigorous discipline that sets them apart from other, less focused collectors.

Above left *Vicente Wolf has the perfect environment in which to display and enjoy his many and varied collections. A large Manhattan loft with windows on three sides means that he can create a series of gallery-like spaces that lead the eye ever onward.*

Above right *As a designer, Wolf understands the importance of visual association. Although this group is predominantly, although not exclusively, Eastern figures, two are Western in style, adding depth and an element of surprise.*

Right *Two collections are combined – photographs and chairs. Each is very different and each complements the other, placed in this minimal setting. The conjunction of the molded plastic armchair with its neighbor, the gilded antique seat, is particularly interesting.*

"wonderful collections have never been premeditated, but have always just evolved... if you go for a set thing, it loses its spontaneity"

THE **NATURALISTS**

The Naturalist collector is really one of nature's inquirers, **fascinated** by and drawn to objects from the **natural world**, whether mineral, flora, or fauna. From shells and fossils to feathers and flowers, the **variety** and **beauty** of natural life is worthy of endless study.

the naturalists are the most instinctive collectors of all, seeking magical elements of the natural world for attention and display

Early collectors were generally interested in subject areas that were contained by one or other of the two great disciplines of arts and sciences. In the arts were ranged the antiquarians and the collectors of pictures, manuscripts, books, and small decorative objects; in the sciences stood those with a keen interest in how the world around them, particularly the natural world, worked and how it might affect their lives.

Those interested in the natural world today are direct descendants of seventeenth-, eighteenth- and nineteenth-century collectors who amassed elements from nature. It was inevitable that collecting in any area that seemed to illuminate an aspect of the natural world became important in previous centuries. Everybody discussed so-called natural wonders, and even sophisticated, educated men made notes in their diaries when they came across pickled or petrified parts. As a result, in many early collections there were things that today seem merely weird and certainly not worthy of exhibition or wonder, "curiosities" that were then carefully documented and displayed. In 1645, the diarist John Evelyn carefully recorded that the collection of a Signor Rugoni of Venice "abounded in things petrified – walnuts, eggs in which the yolk rattled, a pear, a piece of beef with the bones in it and a whole hedgehog." Most wondrous was "a plaice on a wooden trencher turn'd into stone, and very perfect." This careful description uncovers a burgeoning desire to set in place a thorough investigation of every aspect of the living world; nature in all its permutations was of interest – flora and fauna, including birds and insects. Seventeenth-century

Above right *Emma Hawkins has a great fondness for her stuffed animals, and it shows in the artistic and sympathetic way that she displays them in her Edinburgh house. Here in the hall, bird and monkeys engage in a timeless stand-off, refereed by an impartial stag.*

Below right *Off the entrance hall, a pair of eland horns frame the door in an almost neoclassical manner; the antique impression is reinforced by the leopard-legged gilded console table and the patrician bust that presides over the scene from the opposite corner.*

travelers and collectors of botanical curiosities included both of the John Tradescants, father and son. The elder, gardener to King Charles I of England, explored Russia in 1618 and North Africa in 1620, and his son traveled to Virginia in the mid-1600s; both returned with botanical wonders that formed the basis of many influential plant collections.

The eighteenth century saw even more collectors of exotica, but also those who studied with intensity the natural history around them. The most enduringly popular resulting work in English is that of the clergyman Gilbert White, *The Natural History of Selborne*, published in 1789, a minutely detailed account of the natural life of his village and the surrounding Hampshire countryside. This was also a time of growing desire for the systematic, particularly scientific, investigation of nature in the hope that it would reveal a set of both natural and moral laws. The century produced men of the caliber of Sir Joseph Banks, who traveled with Captain James Cook on his round-the-world voyage in 1768–71. After his return to England, Banks became deeply involved with the Royal Gardens at Kew, from where collectors were dispatched to the farthest ends of the earth – western and southern Africa, Australia, China – to bring back new plant specimens.

PASSIONATE NATURAL HISTORIANS

It could be said that the contemporary collectors that we have chosen to call naturalists are the most basic, the most instinctive collectors of all. Perhaps their interest in the natural world is a continuation of the collections of childhood, when the excitement of finding a bird's nest, discarded snakeskin, or perfect shell was almost magical. Shells are just as widely collected today as they ever were. During the eighteenth century, their popularity was such that some collections were considered so impressive and valuable that they were occasionally sold at auction. Mrs. Mary Delany, wife of an Irish dean, collected two sorts of shells – those to be used as decoration (she specialized in designing and making shell grottoes and elaborate shell garlands that

Above left *The delicacy of birds' skeletons, part of an extensive collection, is off-set by the formal, clean lines of the fine broken-pediment, break-front bureau in which they are displayed. On the chair in front, a very-much-alive parrot celebrates his good fortune.*

Below left *Emma Hawkins' genius and imagination in display are shown in the way in which she has used this nineteenth-century sideboard and some glass domes to show off a varied group of objects – most of them natural, but a few just quirky.*

were hung as wall friezes) and those to be studied and admired. In 1743, she wrote: "Sir John has given me some very pretty shells for my works, but none fine enough for my collection; but a friend in the West Indies has promised me great curiosities." And in 1750: "I have been very busy in cleaning my new shells and arranging them in my cabinet, and adding those I brought with me – and now they make a dazzling show." And shells were not just considered pretty little trifles collected only by ladies; they were also collected by virtuosos whose other interests might encompass such high-minded interests as books, medals, and paintings.

One contemporary collector for whom such natural wonders still hold a charm is Parisian Françoise De Nobele. In her top-floor apartment is a magical conglomeration of things natural and not so natural – skeletons, skulls and serpents' heads, all mixed together with manmade representations of nature in different materials. All these rub shoulders with pieces of ethnic art, piles of illustrated and rare books, and twentieth-century ceramics. Her apartment is a true, timeless cabinet of curiosities.

A series of interconnecting rooms opens to reveal stranger and stranger objects. At first sight, there is almost too much to take in – it seems cluttered, a jumble – but gradually the eye begins to differentiate distinct shapes and forms, and to see that everything is there with a purpose and grouped in a

particular way for effect. On one table is a collection of skulls, on another death masks. A third surface is in reptilian guise, with a grasshopper made out of metal and model snakes, and close by is a collection of jawbones and teeth. Behind each group is a background, one a *trompe l'oeil* doorway, its pediment garlanded with wreaths.

Françoise De Nobele says that she does not like apartments that are too sterile or neat, and that textiles do not appeal to her. Green – nature's color – is her preferred shade; not only does it figure on walls and furniture, but each room is also bathed in a green dappled light as the sun filters through a balcony potted up with long-leafed plants and shrubs.

In other hands, so many small skeletons and skulls could be a touch macabre, but her skill in grouping her collection is immediately noticeable. Each object is teamed with confidence, and all are carefully chosen for color and texture. She uses shapes – sinuous shapes – and it is all unbelievably subtle and unusual. Each group thus displayed is a still life, an artistic composition, and an important lesson in the art of grouping a collection.

Collectors of natural objects have a curiosity and fascination not only with nature, but often also with natural laws themselves. Paul Dawson and Harold Galloway have an entire room devoted to natural objects called, unsurprisingly, the "Nature Room." The contents are, as you might imagine, a

million miles away from the average dead and dying examples found in most school nature rooms. Paul and Harold's version of nature is true to the Victorian ideal that all their collections espouse. It was not planned as such; as with many good collections, this group evolved almost by chance. As they added ceramics, pressed flowers, and insects to their other examples of Victorian life, they realized that what they had in front of them was tantamount to a working exhibit illustrating the Victorian passion for information and facts. Everything in this room is of interest – even the verdant wallpaper (by the now defunct company, John Lines), which was chosen to complement the room's collections. Although Paul Dawson jokingly says that it is a room filled with "lots of little dead things," he is deliberately concerned with reflecting the nineteenth-century passion for classification that accompanied the growth of Darwinism. To prove the point, one plate back carries an original label on which is inscribed: "The Darwin theory explained – what is man?" Not surprisingly, no answer is recorded.

Victorian decoration was often a combination of the order and decorative pleasure that are displayed here. Shells in boxes, butterflies pinned by color and type in glass cases, for example, are plentiful in the Nature Room. There is also a wonderful collection of pressed ferns, each arranged so decoratively and so carefully that one is immediately overwhelmed by the variety of pattern and design that the fern family possesses. No manmade pattern could be subtler than those to be found on these individual leaves. There was an eccentric side to the Victorian fascination with the decorative properties of nature as well. Some ceramicists made pots, pitchers and platters with applied creatures and insects crawling all over them, and leaves and forest-floor plants curling around. Paul Dawson says that their own collection of such wares is an integral part of "a cabinet of curiosities in which things challenge one's preconceptions, much as a nineteenth-century collection would have done." And there are, indeed, naturalistic surprises to be found in many a corner display of their collections.

Opposite *So many Victorian passions are recorded here: using shells as decoration – a pastime of eighteenth- and nineteenth-century ladies; elaborate china flowers; and the art of filling glass bell-shaped paperweights with layers of sands showing picturesque views of the Isle of Wight.*

Above left *A flawless sailor's shell Valentine; a lamp with a nautilus shell shade by W.A.S. Benson; stuffed birds and fish; preserved butterflies; and ceramic manifestations of flora and fauna, including an imposing Burmantoft vase and grotesque vases by Blanche Vulliamy, decorate the room.*

Above right *English Bretby naturalistic wares of different leaf forms, with disconcertingly lifelike cookies and nuts attached to them, are displayed in a fine and intricate cabinet decorated with different types of ferns, preserved under varnish.*

WILD LIFE

"Dried animals" are often mentioned in inventories of famous collections of the past, although not so much is said of stuffed ones. Today, however, many collectors appreciate and, indeed, relish the results of the taxidermist's art. Hubert Zandberg, a successful interior decorator in London, has a fascination with the natural world and all its manifestations. He thinks that this derives from his upbringing in South Africa, where nature is impossible to ignore, larger than life and surrounds you like a wraparound cinema screen. As do many of the other naturalist collectors, Hubert Zandberg has several

examples of the taxidermist's art, mainly South African birds and beasts, of which he is very fond. "People have a thing about taxidermy and about nature being perceived in the most contrived way," he comments. "But I feel that if, like me, you grew up with wild animals around you and the first thing that you were taught was to respect wildlife as I was, then it's a completely different way of thinking. Perhaps these stuffed animals do not have the same connotations that they do for others."

Porcupine quills, horns, and tusks; coral and sticks; eggs and shells cover the surfaces of Zandberg's minute apartment. There is a flamingo and a basket of tortoises' shells in the living room; a cockateel and a tiger's head in the bedroom; horns on the floor, and pressed flowers and coral on the walls. There is also something I have never seen before – a pale, preserved shrimp in all its rock-pool glory, displayed like an interesting relic, box-framed and hanging on the wall. Perhaps

"I grew up with wild life all around me, so these stuffed animals do not have the same connotations for me as they do for some"

Top left *There is a beauty in quill and horn, bone and shell that is often best comprehended when seen in as simple a form as possible, so that all the subtle, natural variations can be appreciated at close view.*

Above left *Bleached-out whole tortoise shells have a certain melancholic air, but look very beautiful displayed as a group on a pale background. To bring them into contrast, Zandberg has placed a small African ceremonial cap immediately behind the shells.*

Above *The complete naturalist's group, including the tortoise shells, is shown to be a complex and harmonious display. A sawfish bill gives height at one side of a sepia-toned photograph and is balanced by an ornate cowry-shell headdress on the other.*

Left *In this group, the delicacy of nature can be appreciated and admired. The fragility of a leaf's veining, the airy pallor of a piece of bleached coral, and the nearly translucent body of a small crustacean are all objects of beauty.*

entering the kitchen is like stepping into a field guide: glass-fronted cases of stuffed birds line the walls and owls, auks, and razorbills stare down on you beadily

because the place is so small, you really do get a sense of being in a genuine seventeenth- or eighteenth-century cabinet of curiosities, because all is really very curious indeed.

Another nature lover, Emma Hawkins, lives in a tall, very elegant Regency house in Edinburgh. She has representatives of many branches of the tree of life – particularly those of the bird kingdom. Only one – a chatty parrot – is alive, however; the rest are stuffed and perch on plinths, in display cases, and under glass domes. Entering the kitchen is an Alice-like step into the pages of a field guide to birds: glass-fronted cases of stuffed birds line the walls, and owls, auks, and razorbills stare down beadily from above the range. Emma Hawkins has a fascination with taxidermy and – like other lovers of the

inanimate – finds the idea enjoyable, rather than repellent. A true naturalist, she also collects other parts of animals and displays them in a most un-museumlike way. An immense whale bone stands on a round hall table, like an ultracontemporary piece of modern sculpture. Instead of embroidered silk bellpulls, sawfish bills hang either side of the drawing-room fireplace. Delicate small birds' skulls arranged together on a low table look like polished ivory carvings, and an elephant's skull on the floor masquerades as a large, uncomfortable stool. The precision and detail with which she arranges everything throughout the house makes the elements of her entire collection look less like natural phenomena and far more like examples of fine craft and design.

Above left *On a pair of matching cabinets, birds in glass cases flank a portrait of Mona Guthrie, painted by St. John Helier Lander, that is hung over the fireplace. On the floor, a game bird struts his stuff, albeit confined within his glass case.*

Above right *Sawfish bills emphasize the high gilded mirror; antique boxed collections of shells sit on tables; and coral and giant clam shells are used as ornament – altogether a perfect example of how to integrate natural curiosities into a domestic, traditional setting.*

Right *On the table is a wooden dish of cricket balls, well polished on many a pair of white flannel slacks; on the wall behind hang a camel and a buffalo skull, together with a swooping bird. Feathers and dried branches make an alternative flower arrangement.*

Laurent Dombrowicz and Franck Delmarcelle also include pieces that display several aspects of the natural world as part of their wide-ranging collections. Stuffed animals are, in fact, among their favorite possessions, and their reasons for collecting in this area are endearing. "Taxidermy is about curiosities, not about theater," they explain. "It's strange that although we love animals – we live in hunting country, for example, and yet we are very against the hunt – we also love these trophies. We certainly don't want to kill animals, but when it has already been done, we feel that by collecting them, these specimens are saved for eternity – and are even in some ways still alive. You could say that when we find stuffed animals at a flea market, we almost think we must save them and give them a better life here, where they can be together with all the others." The stuffed animals somehow take up their rightful places as cohabitants of Dombrowicz's and Delmarcelle's home.

Above left *A curious family, but a family nonetheless, is convened in these examples of the taxidermist's art in Laurent Dombrowicz and Frank Delmarcelle's farmhouse in northern France. Perhaps they look so much at home because of the respect and affection their owners feel for them.*

Top right *Many of us do not immediately notice the natural beauty of a shell. It was not always the case: in the eighteenth century, shells – especially rare ones – were highly valued. Looking at these exquisite specimens, one can understand why.*

Above right *Fossils and ammonites have always held a fascination for the curious, for it is difficult to comprehend that such decorative specimens are many thousands of years old. Perhaps their intricacy means that they are best displayed in simple fashion.*

Right *Where better to show an aquatic collection than close to water? In Delmarcelle and Dombrowicz's bathroom, the antique free-standing bathtub is raised on a wooden platform and surrounded by oversized shells and pieces of coral.*

Below right *Elsewhere in the bathroom, the marine collection is grouped together with pieces of classical and funerary art; the connection is evident – the forms and motifs of each are to be seen in abundance in classical art.*

NATURE'S DECORATIVE ARTS

The moment that you step inside his apartment, it is evident that Peter Adler is a born collector. "From childhood, I was a collector," he admits, "of bottles, stamps, seashells. Now that I am older, I find that I put all my energies into collecting certain things and then move on to something else. At the moment I am very interested in rock crystals and fossils." These can be seen all around the main room, alongside seashells and semiprecious stones. Throughout the apartment, these pieces of natural art are displayed as though they were decorative objects. On the floor is a large bowl of tiny, polished, rock-crystal eggs, cold to the touch, and irresistible to hold; on a low table, a group of ammonites, semiprecious stones sliced through the center, and small fossils are displayed together. These are things to be picked up and admired, not gazed at from afar.

Hunt Slonem also combines his naturalist talents with a highly refined artistic sense. Nature is everywhere in his Manhattan studio – not just in trees and plants in tubs, bright jungle canvases or real parrots flying around and chattering in your ear, but also in collections of shells, butterflies, and all things beautiful. Two giant clams are filled with cowrie shells; a dish of pale pink shells is grouped with miniature Parian busts; and a glass table-display case is crammed with large shells as a base for a multicolored group of flasks. In a vibrant red room, one wall is entirely covered with cases of butterflies that might have been the envy of earlier enthusiasts.

Naturalist collectors have retained a sense of wonder in the natural world that many of us lose after childhood. They appreciate the beauty of a butterfly's wing, the curve of a tusk, and the pattern of a shell. They are also adept at the art of using and displaying their natural treasures in a way that reminds the rest of us how to appreciate their artistic qualities and their scientific value and wonder.

Right *Artist Hunt Slonem incorporates natural pieces into his decorative interior schemes. In this room, color is the outward link; on the table, larger and smaller shells are combined with glass and ceramic shapes to form a shell-pink tableau.*

Below *Demonstrating that decorative excellence can come from both natural and applied art, Hunt Slonem – in a room of lipstick red – combines butterfly boxes with his own paintings, assorted shells, and a small collection of Parian busts.*

THE **UTILITARIANS**

The Utilitarian collector is one who sees
beauty in the commonplace, and who
revels in the **practical** and familiar objects
that are a necessary part of our daily lives.
From rolling pins to radiators,
the Utilitarian appreciates and understands
the **pure simplicity** of function and form.

H ave nothing in your houses that you do not know to be useful, or believe to be beautiful," wrote William Morris, one of the founders of the Arts and Crafts Movement. The year was 1882, and I make no excuse for appropriating here such a well-known quotation, for it could justifiably be claimed as the rallying cry of that honest man, the utilitarian collector.

Of course, long before Morris's time, many people had as much appreciation for the useful and practical as they ever had for the decorative and ornamental. Scientific instruments, for example, had been collected since they were first made; and every sort of engine and its multiple components have long had an intriguing hold over a large section of the population. This is understandable, because it would be hard for anyone not to appreciate, say, the beauty of the workings of a clock – particularly when the design and ornamentation of the unseen parts are given as much attention as the case.

Just because something is useful does not mean to say that it is neither beautiful nor fun. Many utilitarians take a pleasure in the basics of life and consider their collections close to a form of contemporary art. If you like good design, you will understand the allure of the utilitarian and the everyday. Design is all about form and function and the beauty of texture and patina. The skeins of twine, balls of string, and hanks of rope that Hubert Zandberg has piled into a basket are just as beautiful to many as a piece of hand-painted porcelain. Collecting the utilitarian also shows an appreciation of useful art. The weathervanes collected by Jerry and Susan Lauren could not be more utilitarian, but few would fail to appreciate their beauty.

EVERYDAY BEAUTY

In many ways, Charles Paget Wade was the arch utilitarian. Born in 1883, when there was still a widespread knowledge and appreciation of the crafts of daily life, Wade was a collector of the mundane and the exotic. He wrote that he "bought things not because they were rare or valuable – there are many things of everyday use in the past, of small value, but of interest as records of various vanished handicrafts." His guiding essentials for any piece were workmanship, tone, and design, exemplified by his wonderful collection of iron objects. All of them are utilitarian and beautiful – such as keys, hand bells, hinges, and locks. Door hardware has, in fact, since the Renaissance been valued; the greatest metal workers of the time felt it was no disgrace to design and make such everyday pieces.

Below *This is an illustration of how a collection can be formed from the most utilitarian of objects. Pieces of antique hardware gain a new impact and significance when grouped closely together in a way that allows insight into the craft.*

Wade's first purchases for Snowshill were nearly all household items – from lace bobbins to a hand loom and a collection of spinning wheels; he also collected essential ships' instruments, such as chronometers and telescopes. Still to be seen in the house today is his collection of bicycles – penny farthings, boneshakers, and an 1820 hobby-horse (a bicycle without pedals, but with elbow- and foot-rests). They are kept in the attic, some hanging from the ceiling, others ranged against the floor, where together they make a pattern of intertwining spheres. Utilitarians appreciate the workmanship that lies behind an object, and Wade was no exception: he collected tools of every variety, even bringing

home the complete contents of a Suffolk cobbler's shop.

One of the problems with being a utilitarian is that many desirable objects are big – really big – and you need enough room to store and display them. In lieu of an empty English manor house such as that of Charles Paget Wade, a Manhattan loft may do as well. Certainly, artist Hunt Slonem, who conveniently has not one Manhattan loft, but two, would agree. In one of his studio-lofts is displayed a collection of that most useful of objects – the chair. Chairs are good examples of how the everyday can be rearranged as a collection that shows the intrinsic lines, the art and thought, behind the objects, not to mention a visual history of furniture design. Hunt Slonem likes to collect gothic chairs – not the originals, but rather examples of the nineteenth-century enthusiastic rediscovery of medieval art. He has collected them over a long period of time, and each is very

different – high, low, elaborate, or relatively simple. They include three immense examples known as the Jones chairs, which came originally from the house of a wealthy and acquisitive Mr. Jones, who once gave his name to the expression "keeping up with the Joneses." Big spaces make for big ideas and complementing the chairs are two enormously oversized sofas – one once owned by Gloria Vanderbilt, the other by Andy Warhol – that almost constitute a grand twentieth-century collection in themselves.

FUNCTIONAL ART

Hunt Slonem's sofas may be large, but at least their practical purpose is easy to define. This is not always the case with utilitarians' finds. Glen Senk and Keith Johnson collect industrial pieces that were once massively functional, objects that are overpowering in a marvelously original way. It helps that their house

Above *As if awaiting a convocation of ghostly kings, Hunt Slonem's Victorian Gothic chairs sit silently around an oversized table, arranged in such a way that the differences in scale and variations in ornament can be enjoyed.*

Left *Sandwiched between Hunt Slonem's two oversized sofas is part of his collection of American glass – most of it made by a factory called Blenko in the mid-twentieth century. His painting behind makes a stupendous background.*

outside Philadelphia is large and airy, with wide-open rooms through which the light streams. The pieces they like to have about them have a sculptural quality; they have metamorphosed from the purely functional, becoming art installations in their own right.

Although many utilitarians collect the domestic and the useful, few display their collections in the imaginative, breathtaking manner of Senk and Johnson. They have no fear of the large or otherwise daunting, an issue that might concern a more fainthearted collector. Like the participants and audience at the Great Exhibition in London of 1851, they revel in the glory of the industrial. They can see the decorative possibilities in such unlikely things as a cowshed floor, roof finials, and wrought-iron gates. The gates – from a school or

Below left *In Glen Senk and Keith Johnson's Philadelphia home, pieces of architectural exterior decoration are displayed as ornamental objects in their own right; grouped together against the wooden panels of the stairs, the wooden curlicues and fretwork patterns make a strong design statement.*

Below right *Contained in a panel on the wall of the hall are four large French metal panels originally designed to be used as teaching aids for student drivers. With their clear, simplistic graphics, they make an amusing and original picture.*

college – are wall-hung in heraldic mode on each side of a door. What appears at first glance to be the most unpromising of all their finds – a section of a dimpled cowshed floor – is hung behind a long wooden table, pulling the two together as sculptural pieces of art. Another three-dimensional object, a brass and metal radiator, is also hung center stage on a wall; displayed like this you appreciate the work and the design in a way that transcends its more recognizable function.

Their Brobdingnag tendencies do not stop them from enjoying collecting and arranging the small and much used, such as brushes and spools of thread. In an upstairs room, a collection of paint brushes – as utilitarian as you can get – is arranged in neat lines on a deep windowsill, where they take on a charm and a life of their own. So do the paint-smeared palettes over the fireplace, and the display of old reels of cord, grouped together with a pyramid of rolls of braid and ribbon.

Above left *The most ordinary of objects can look decorative when well displayed. Here a collection of old, well-used paint palettes are grouped together, with the witty addition of a small painting of a palette and paint brushes.*

Left *Probably the most unlikely object to be found in this book, part of an old cowshed floor, is treated with as much attention – and looks as good – as many a more conventional piece of contemporary art.*

Right *The intrinsic beauty of a purely functional object is well demonstrated by this vintage metal radiator, which has been treated as a piece of sculpture and displayed in a prominent, eye-catching position.*

unlikely objects from the collection, such as a cowshed floor, roof finials, a vintage radiator, and wrought-iron gates, are transformed into imaginative installations that take center stage in a Philadelphia house

A different genus of utilitarian collectors are those whose collections spring wholly from their work. In the Massachusetts house of designers Walter and Ise Gropius, every teacup or cooking pan was part of their collection and of the overall decorative plan of the house. A unifying color scheme that applied throughout the house was applied to the household articles – which were all in white, gray, and earth tones, slashed by occasional red highlights.

The Gropius' kitchen became a means to an intellectually satisfying end via its relationship to the dining area, rather than being a space for particular design attention beyond the functional. The open-plan dining room was designed so that food and utensils could travel back and forth without interruption to the conversation of the diners. The dining table, designed for six people and with a white formica top, was an integral part of the collection, displaying dramatic black and white tablewares that complemented the design themes of the room. The lighting was also carefully considered so it would display the dishes and glasses to best effect: an industrial recessed ceiling spotlight, at that time used only in musuems and art galleries, was installed above the dining table, masked to adjust to whatever reflected shape was needed on the table below.

The most functional objects of all, the furniture, are today considered to constitute an important collection, a chronology of original and factory pieces designed by Marcel Breuer. They range from lightweight tubular steel chairs and tables conceived at the Bauhaus workshops, to a plywood laminate chair designed for the Isokon company in England. Even the smallest furnishing details, such as the filing cabinets and special lamps produced in the metal workshops in Dessau, were carefully considered parts of an interior collection.

This page *In one sense, everything in Walter Gropius's house represents a celebration and a collection of the utilitarian. The curved lines of this teaset, made by Rosenthal and admired by Ise and Walter Gropius, is a fine example of functional beauty.*

Above right *In the Gropius house, where everything is placed for a purpose, it is often difficult to separate the functional from the ornamental. Even the internal glass brick wall, as utilitarian as it could be, has a certain translucent beauty.*

Below right *These small bentwood stools by the fire in the Gropius living room were designed by Yanagi in Tokyo in 1925. Although completely functional, there is a swooping beauty to them that gives them a sculptural quality.*

Below far right *In Ise and Walter's daughter's room, function takes place over ornament. The bedside table was made in the Bauhaus workshops in Dessau in 1925, and the lamp, like all the others in the house, is American, bought in 1937 from industrial suppliers.*

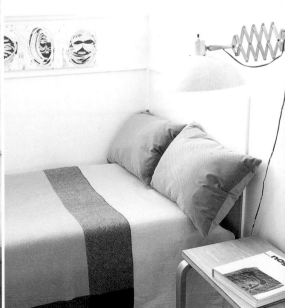

Top *For Diane de Clercq, knitwear designer with her sister Evelyne, the functional is the decorative, and vice versa. Here, beside an antique wooden dressmaker's mannequin, is another in miniature, dressed in a tiny version of one of de Clercq's designs.*

Above *Woven squares, executed on a tiny hand machine, of some of the trial samples of woolen color combinations that the sisters use in their work are now displayed as panels of texture and color in their studio in the middle of Rome.*

Left *Behind the desk is a wonderful framed display of each of the knitwear designs, in miniature, that have been produced over twenty-five years. The idea is an incomparable filing system of past design work.*

Below *But is it art? The perennial decorative allure of the painter's palette finds expression in the de Clercq studio, with each one artistically arranged here in a display that is not as haphazard as it may first appear.*

Diane de Clercq is a knitwear designer of much talent, who is based in Rome. "Everything here is connected with work, with design," she says of her home. "The display of pieces follows naturally on. I do have themes to my collecting, but it is not a studied idea – rather, it is organic." One of her collections is both individual and intimately connected with her work – a display case of minute knitted sweaters, one from every collection she has designed over the last twenty-five years. "I always made them," she says, "and they represent my collecting life. The pieces are not dated – I can remember the date of each one, and why I designed that particular pattern. They are not just a collection of my past, but also an inspiration." This, in one sense, is collecting at its best, where not only are the objects a pleasure to look at, but they also have a significance to the owner that goes beyond mere display.

Below *Part of the de Clercq collection of hat molds, in which each is different and looks like a large piece of turned treen. A single one would not have the same impact – it is in a group that their form and past function can be properly appreciated.*

these are not just acquisitions to be counted and arranged, but living reminders of other times, other traditions, and of other, original users

In her studio is a small grouping of colored wool stripes, each one woven in a different combination: "I see new combinations all the time. I make tiny palettes. They become a collection of the mind." On another side of the studio is a collection of the most surprising, life-sized children's dress patterns made from heavy brown paper. She found them in a market in Kenya, where they are cut from old produce sacks. Every last pocket and ruffle is sewn on in paper, and they hang by the stand, beside different piles of material and a sewing machine. The customer chooses a design and

the fabric, and returns in an hour to pick up the finished dress. Elsewhere is a collection of the polished wooden shoe lasts and hat molds that she buys whenever she sees them. It is the shapes and the textures of the wood that interest her, and also the way that the shapes of the shoe lasts, in particular, are so evocative of past styles and types of shoe. Perhaps this collection contains a sum of the charms appreciated by the utilitarians. For them, the objects of their collections are not just acquisitions to be counted and arranged, but living reminders of other times, other traditions, and the people who used them.

Above *Three of the evocative sample children's paper dress patterns found by Diane de Clercq hanging by a stand in a market in Kenya are displayed here in frames.*

This page *In front of a dress pattern made from a paper maize sack are pieces from the collection of shoe lasts – each one so different from the next, testament to the variety of shoe shapes in fashion and to the idiosyncracies of human feet.*

THE **ENTHUSIASTS**

The Enthusiast collector is that **sympathetic** character, the all-rounder, who cannot resist **accumulating** everything and anything that appeals. Imaginative and **artistic**, Enthusiasts are always on the brink of another collection to keep them enthralled – until **inspiration** strikes anew.

Left *The lines of these two tubular steel chairs, designed by Marcel Breuer in the 1920s, appear as contemporary today as when they were first produced. They are still manufactured, but the early versions are highly sought-after and command high prices.*

Right *Vicente Wolf really is an enthusiast collector. His work as an international interior decorator means that he is constantly exposed to new ideas and interests. Here a selection from his photography collection is simply displayed in his New York apartment.*

Enthusiasts are prone to collecting everything and anything, from furniture to books, artefacts to scientific instruments. The sky quickly becomes the limit – in fact, if you could collect different types of sky, some enthusiast, somewhere, would be doing so. And although no one enthusiast collects the same as another, they all have in common the fact that there is no knowing – even by them – what they will collect next.

Renaissance thinkers, epitomized, perhaps, by Leonardo da Vinci, were as interested in science as in art in an era that did not make the distinctions we now do between the two disciplines. For example, da Vinci produced designs for an early form of flight and devised an irrigation system for the plains of Lombardy. By the seventeenth and eighteenth centuries, it was accepted that every man of education would have a curiosity in anything to do with what might be loosely classified as the sciences – both natural and otherwise. Subjects worthy of debate and study ranged from botany to the alchemist's search – via the philosopher's stone – for gold, and included medicine, geology, engineering, and mechanics.

In the seventeenth century, Ashmole was certainly one of the first documented collectors of objects that touched scientific and natural interests – minerals, insects, fish, and other animals. He added to his collections all the time, often buying from the collections of others, so that his own constantly grew in size and numbers. This syndrome was demonstrated in the eighteenth century by, for example, the Duchess of Portland. Her interest in all natural things, and botany in particular, was complemented by a collection of heraldic bindings, rare folios, miniatures, and antique medals.

The Rothschild family were particularly party to such wide-ranging collecting habits. Many of the fruits can be seen today at Waddesdon Manor in Buckinghamshire, built by Baron Ferdinand de Rothschild in the late 1800s and lived in by several generations of the family. Ferdinand filled the house with such treasures as porcelain and gold boxes and a collection of particularly fine eighteenth-century French furniture. His sister, Miss Alice, with whom he lived after the death of his wife, was also an inveterate collector, who managed by the time of her death to fill not only Waddesdon, but also two other houses, with pictures and furniture. Even the ornamental dairy in the grounds of Waddesdon was home to a collection, which included Kändler models of Dresden animals and birds, ancient examples of faience, and other suitably rustic curiosities. The house is a testament to the collecting abilities and mania of the Rothschild family, and the fact that the phrase *le gout Rothschild* is well understood in antique circles is a testament to their enthusiast identity.

Furniture collecting in the late nineteenth century was for serious enthusiasts, such as the new millionaires of America, including the greatest collector of all, J. Pierpont Morgan. Today, although fine antique furniture is still collected, there is also a more eclectic view of the genre. The benchmark does not have to be that espoused by Rothschilds, Vanderbilts, and

piles of books are everywhere –
new ones, old folios, and rare
works – replacing stools and tables,
almost engulfing the apartment

Morgans. Many enthusiasts collect certain types of furniture – particularly chairs – in which the style and design somehow sum up the enthusiast's brief. Both Vicente Wolf and Hunt Slonem collect chairs – with Wolf basing his choice on shape and Slonem narrowing the choice down to chairs designed in Gothic style. Traditional collecting enthusiasts would have numbered paintings along with furniture. Although paintings are still widely collected, many enthusiasts prefer to collect photography – the modern equivalent of an earlier vogue, perhaps. Vicente Wolf is an avid collector: "I have been collecting photographs for twenty years. It was Richard Avedon who suggested that I start; he remarked that too often people never see what is in front of them. I found that thought interesting, so of course I started to look. I went to auctions and museums until I knew what I was looking at."

BIBLIOMANIA

The sort of things that we have around us on a daily basis, such as books, have always been venerated by collectors. Rich men of taste, in particular, amassed books and drawings on art and architecture, which were housed in specially built libraries. When books were comparatively rare – and correspondingly expensive – they were treated as precious objects. Books were not kept in glazed cases until the end of the seventeenth century; Samuel Pepys is thought to have had one of the first such pieces of furniture, certainly one of the first depicted. Richard Heber, born in 1773, was a great bibliophile; for him, book collecting dominated all else, and his descendant Osbert Sitwell said that his dictum was that "no gentleman can be without three copies of a book, one for show, one for use, and one for borrowers." After his death in 1833, it

was discovered that he had filled eight houses with books, "overflowing all the rooms, chairs, tables and passages." He probably owned between 127,000 and 146,000, and they took three years to disperse at auction. J. Pierpont Morgan, who only ever bought the best, owned a copy of the Gutenberg Bible, as well as thirty-two books printed by Caxton.

Enthusiasts love the tactile quality of books, as well as their visual beauty, and enjoy the great variety of printed works – ancient books, manuscripts, books printed on private presses, illustrated books, modern first editions, and authors' proofs, for instance. Many collectors do specialize, but others simply can't decide and just buy everything and anything that interests them. Françoise De Nobele's book collection threatens to engulf her apartment. Piles of books are everywhere – new ones, old folios, and rare works – taking the place of stools

and tables, with objects from others of her collections perched precariously on top. Belgian decorator Agnès Emery also loves her books, but she does not treat them haphazardly. Instead, they are color coded on shelves, and when the bindings do not fit her color scheme, they are re-covered accordingly.

Armor and weapons were also collected by earlier enthusiasts, particularly in the nineteenth century, when collectors were seduced by the romance of popular novels, such as Sir Walter Scott's *Rob Roy*. In the last century, Charles Paget Wade filled many walls at Snowshill with arms and armor. In fact, the house is a veritable shrine to enthusiasm. The Music Room does not just house a single piano or harpsichord, but is full of musical instruments – violins, harps, trumpets, and even a triangle from the local troupe of Morris Men. Ship models and ship paraphernalia are everywhere: one room is named Mizzen, another Topgallant. Children's toys are kept in a room called Seventh Heaven.

Above left *Perhaps the greatest enthusiast of all time was twentieth-century collector Charles Paget Wade. Every room in his house was filled – literally from floor to ceiling – with his finds, such as this eclectic mix of model ships, pictures, drums, and a globe.*

Left *In the Priest's House, where Wade lived, the ground floor was dominated by the old hall-porter's chair, in which Wade would listen to his battery-driven "wireless" radio. Most of the objects here are English domestic and farm tools.*

Right *In the Music Room, the instruments, which have been arranged approximately in the form of a small orchestra or band, include an eighteenth-century three-stringed double bass and two cellos, as well as two Irish harps, banjos, and a hurdy-gurdy.*

Left *Hunt Slonem collects glass candlesticks. He is not looking for pairs, or a particular shape or color, but simply for those made of glass. And when he has found one, he adds it to the others marching down his long table, and they look wonderful.*

Right *Slonem also collects other types of glass – carafes, decanters, pitchers – in every possible shape and color, many made by the American company Blenko, but some from Italian glassmakers. As the man says: "I'm not a minimalist."*

Below *His artist's eye means that much of the impact of his glass collections comes through the way he relates them by color. Here he has grouped together cranberry and purple glass, and for depth, placed them against a purple velvet sofa.*

DECORATIVE AND EVOCATIVE

Glass makes a colorful collection, perhaps as an acceptable adult version of children's toys, complete with the same shiny brightness and eccentricity of shape. Hunt Slonem collects what is known as "Blenko" glass. Originally made in the United States in the 1920s – and once easy to find, cheap and cheerful – the pieces are now elusive and expensive. "As with so much Americana," explains Hunt, "when I started to collect four years ago it cost between $80 and $100 a piece, but it is about $1200 today." In case the supply of Blenko runs out, Slonem also collects Italian glass of a similar nature and range of bright colors. Although it seems a superfluous comment, he adds that he is not a minimalist collector. "I can't stand empty space," he says. To that end, he groups his glass collection in blocks of color against the large loft windows, all to spectacular effect.

"outlandish" was once a word used in admiration of the more unusual collecting enthusiasms – a tradition continued today by some devotees

Above left *In Françoise De Nobele's apartment is a scene like a surrealist aquarium: starfish play around trees of coral, some of which are real, some manmade in other materials. From a coral branch hang miniature carved skulls and an ivory leg.*

Above right *In this still life (or should that be a no-life?), two skulls lie on a pile of suitably titled books; one skull, in a reminder of glories past, is garlanded with gilded laurels.*

Below right *The seahorse always seems one of the most curious and touching of creatures. Here a dried specimen has been given prominence by suspending him, with a ribbon, in front of a pen and sepia ink drawing.*

Many enthusiasts are keen to collect things that have a link, however spurious, with fame, objects that were either owned, worn, touched, or that otherwise came into contact with someone well known of their time, such as autographed letters. It sometimes seems that both Queens Elizabeth I and Marie Antoinette must have had at least three hands each if the number of gloves purporting to belong to one or other that are still displayed and venerated today is to believed. Elias Ashmole listed Henry VIII's dog's collar in his inventory, and Horace Walpole owned such wondrous, if disconnected, pieces as Cardinal Wolsey's red hat, combs belonging to Elizabeth I and Mary, Queen of Scots, and one that King Charles I used for his wig. He also had a small clock that belonged to Anne Boleyn, the chair of a high priest, and a five hundred year-old chair made of the Glastonbury thorn. And today, when celebrity sales are rife, the wish to collect – perhaps to connect

Above left *One of Françoise De Nobele's new collecting enthusiasms is pottery from the 1950s. Piled up by the fireplace is a group of pitchers, ashtrays, and dishes by Vallauris.*

Below left *An object-lesson in the art of surprise as an essential part of the display of collections is evident in this group. No one part is obvious – not the bust by Henri de Waroquier, the grotesque pitcher, the coral, or the skull.*

Above right *A wide view of the dining room shows that although there are so many different small and unexpected groupings of objects here, the overall impression is one of a pleasant, interesting, and comfortable space.*

– seems to be stronger. Even a collector as sophisticated as David Gill presently counts among his prized possessions a pair of actress and singer Madonna's shoes, displayed in his living room as though they were a piece of sculpture.

It is not only unusual and specific objects that are made the subjects of a collection. Ashmole had listed in his inventory "figures and stories neatly carved on plum stones" and a purse made from toad skin. People have always been interested in the oddities of life, the truly curious, those pieces that have the "well-I-never!" factor. "Outlandish" was a word used not in disapproval, but almost in admiration during the seventeenth and eighteenth centuries, and belief and educated knowledge were suspended for the duration of the view. Françoise De Nobele has some such strange objects – tiny skulls carved out of ivory, a jawbone set in silver. She has an

inspiration beyond the idea of specifically collecting something; themes impose themselves, and if something pleases her, she buys it. She is always in advance of everyone else's taste, and the sum of her collections becomes more extraordinary the closer you look, even to the collector herself. "I let myself be surprised," she says, "I do it for the pleasure." Starting with a color or a style, she groups and regroups the things that come into her apartment by family, in order to "continue a story". It might be chunky ceramic art of the 1950s or delicate creamware; it might be the books or natural or quasi-natural curiosities.

Into this category for the curious and the truly unusual comes the passion for religious art that many enthusiasts share. Françoise De Nobele has some religious pieces interspersed among all the other curiosities, as do Michael Coorengel and Jean Pierre Calvagrac. Laurent

Left *Religious statuary, relics, reliquaries, and other objects pertaining to mortality intrigue Laurent Dombrowicz and Frank Delmarcelle. A winged nineteenth-century St. George, complete with lights, prevents his foe the dragon from entering the living room beyond.*

Below *A pair of bisque angels, designed as funeral ornament, is combined with two other tiny angelic funerary pieces. Along with candlesticks of very different heights, they are subtly displayed against a screen covered with faded eighteenth-century toile.*

Dombrowicz and Franck Delmarcelle entertain even more of a passion for the subject, collecting not only religious statuary that comes originally from churches and burial grounds, but also memorial hair pictures, displayed in a group on the study wall. They also collect reliquaries and relics contained in ornamental caskets, which they display in groups that often combine horns, bones, and stuffed animals. They are intrigued by Masonic art, which may seem antithetical, but which shares many similarities, including preoccupations with death and love.

Perhaps the collector who sums up the idea of the pure enthusiast most completely is Charles de Selliers. There is a coherent theme to his collecting, which seems to be to buy anything that is disliked and neglected by other people. The pieces he lives with, which

religious statuary and memorial trinkets have strong associations with love and death, evoking emotions long past

This page *A complicated but satisfying group is partly religious, partly concerned with death. Everything, from skulls to marbles and pictures, is grouped together in a way that is harmonious and in scale, worthy of the most fastidious of curiosity collectors.*

are stacked high on storage shelves waiting to be seen, are in his view those that no one else would want. Recently, decorative art of the mid-twentieth century has become sought after in some quarters, although not in others. Brought up with traditional collecting tastes, de Selliers has moved on to surround himself with all that is the antithesis of eighteenth-century cultured life. His house in Brussels is filled with art and artifacts of the twentieth and twenty-first centuries – some pieces are commissioned from living artists; others he has tracked down or merely acquired.

De Selliers' house is a testament to the skills of the two people who have been involved in its design – his collecting of

Right *Everything in this room is part of a theme of 1950's popular culture. Here a seemingly disparate group, including a china leopard, an electrified wire sculpture, a robot, and a tin train, are all united beneath a poster for that enduring figurehead of Belgian culture – Tin Tin.*

Below right *Agnès Emery displays pieces in a way that forces you to notice them and therefore appreciate each one individually. A train set, a metal fish, and a clanking automaton are below another Tin Tin poster, and on the floor is a life-size plastic poodle on wheels.*

Below *In the kitchen, a decorative corner is in muted blues and greens, some of Agnès Emery's favorite colors. Painted metal chairs are arranged around an iron table and on shelves above are a combination of 1950's pieces, glasses, and some ceramic bowls designed by Emery.*

Right *It is color and the combination of styles that tells. Against a deep terracotta wall, on a heavy black marble fireplace, is an arrangement of 1950s glass and ceramics. The composition is masterful and always witty – a pair of low Chinese chairs make a seat for an elegant dog.*

Below right *These are strange bed- or shelf-fellows, but because so much care has been taken in the choice of the pieces, such disparate objects as a painted bust of the Madonna, a chunky fish, and the curves of classic 1950's ceramics all work very well together.*

nothing is neglected by the true enthusiast – even the kitsch and the curious can find new life and new coherence in careful design hands

Below right *The bathroom is an example of how function can, and should, be combined with imagination. It is an underwater symphony: aqua tones predominate, with fishy tiles designed by Emery, river-green walls and, to continue the theme, an oversized fish.*

all that, to many, is ugly but interesting, and decorator Agnès Emery's clever grouping and refined color sense. All the very varied pieces from the collection have been brilliantly put together by her, using her particular palette of paint colors as a background and her great gift for arranging even the most disparate objects. She has transformed this collection of the kitsch and the curious by grouping different pieces into stories of color, shape or texture to give them coherence. Some of the groups, particularly those of figures, even

appear to be communicating, having a conversation. On every floor of the house there are many ceramics – in every room and on every surface – some of uncompromising design. There are figures and animals in colored glass and metal; and there are toys, some metal and some plastic, some for adult appreciation and some still used, such as the circular model railroad. De Selliers' collection is now at an end, but who knows where such an enthusiast might go next? The decorative arts of the Louis XV period, perhaps?

THE **DECORATORS**

The Decorator collector is that **talented** person who has the ability to invest every collection – no matter how unpromising – with interest and **charm**. And when it comes to display, where the less perceptive proceed with caution, the Decorator designs with **consummate** style.

Above left *Ogden Codman Jr.'s, influence on his house was enormous. He altered the dark, overcrowded interiors of the 1860s, letting in the light and making it a place of space and air. Two busts, one of Psyche by Hiram Powers, stand either side of the drawing-room window.*

Below left *This wonderful lacquered cabinet had been in the family for many years, but Ogden Codman Jr., repositioned it in the re-modeled morning room, displaying it simply, and to best advantage, in a corner against the plain white, paneled walls.*

Although not many collectors are decorators by profession, very many decorators are collectors by inclination. And why wouldn't they be? Who could resist the dual temptations of constantly being surrounded by interesting, rare, and strange objects and of spending much of your working life being paid to go shopping? Added to these physical temptations is the natural desire of every decorator to arrange, group, and play with objects, rooms, and spaces. In fact, it would be amazing if there is any decorator living who does not collect something.

When decorators become collectors, it is imperative for them to group their objects in attractive ways, often combining them with something else – either another collection or contrasting, interesting objects. They can't not do so: their instincts are for telling stories, as many as possible and preferably all at the same time. In many cases, the sorts of objects that decorators are drawn to are unsurprisingly those that have a strong visual appeal. There can't be many decorators working today who collect, say, stamps or coins, although equally, there are many decorators who could make an attractive and interesting display of either of these.

THE DECORATOR'S EYE

The decorator-collector is not a particularly new phenomenon. Ogden Codman, who is often thought of as one of the first decorators in the modern sense, wrote *The Decoration of Houses* with Edith Wharton over a hundred years ago. He applied himself to his family's collection with a zeal that was unusual in the nineteenth century, displaying and rearranging the house's various treasures so they could be seen in a contemporary light. Many of the collections he was working with had already been built up by either his parents or his grandparents. Codman's skill was to bring the twentieth century into the family house, to let light and air into the rooms and into the collections, and in so doing to give them both an emphasis and a strength that they had not hitherto been able to attain.

This page *Throughout the house, he repositioned various doors and mantels that had been moved or taken out. In the morning room, he used white paint on the walls and replaced the heavy hangings with the freshness of toile de Jouy.*

Left *The dressing area of Walter and Ise Gropius's bedroom is separated off by a glass partition. This simple idea provides the maximum light throughout, while allowing for the different temperatures required in each part of the room as a whole.*

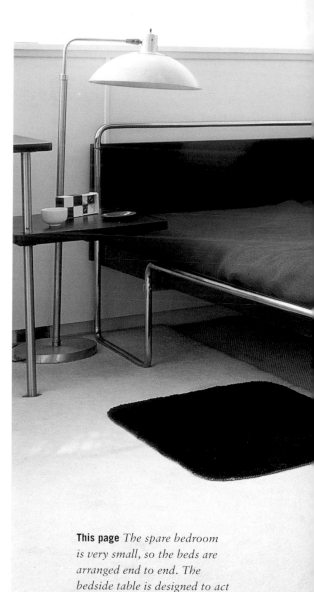

This page *The spare bedroom is very small, so the beds are arranged end to end. The bedside table is designed to act as a night table or, in the day, to swing under the long table of which it is part, to act as a shelf.*

When designing and decorating his Massachusetts house in 1937, light and air were not so much priorities for Walter Gropius as they were essentials. Impressed by the design of American colonial houses that incorporated features to combat the extremes of temperature in New England, he determined to build a house that would reflect their traditions, but that would also be an example of Bauhaus design thinking. Before beginning the building work, he and his wife Ise plotted which way the windows should face in order to take best advantage of the light and views; and they worked out the spatial interior ratios that would be needed in order to incorporate their existing collection of Bauhuas furniture, shipped over from Germany.

They designed the ground, living floor as one large room, divided into three parts, for dining, living, and study. The first two areas were sectioned off by a curtain, and the division between dining and study areas was marked by a wall of glass bricks. Large windows to the west and south allowed fine views. Upstairs, three bedrooms, one with a glass-partitioned dressing room, are naturally lit with ribbon windows that run east and south to give constant light without affecting the interior temperature. Neutral colors are used throughout the house: white, off-white, gray, and black. They allow the clean lines of the outstanding collection of furniture and the important collection of twentieth-century art to be displayed to best effect.

PERFECT BALANCE

Edward Zajac and Richard Callahan know all about emphasis and strength. In a sense they are the ultimate decorator-collectors, because they decorate as they collect and collect as they decorate. What they don't collect, they make or have made, and then add the pieces to one of the existing collections. Their very lives are a decoration: in their Manhattan apartment, which is not large, the scale and verve of their arrangements and displays are breathtaking. The home is a veritable Hall of Mirrors – some of which were designed by the 1930s Parisian jewelry designer Line Vautrin, and some of which were designed in the same mode by Zajac and Callahan. This collection of mirrors dominates the apartment. "They are used as walls, as ornaments, as light reflectors," says Zajac, and proof of their ability to display without dominating is evident in an overall effect that provides vistas and perspective, and manages to be both magical and interesting, rather than chilly and unfriendly. Zajac and Callahan are selective, but in their own way, as Edward Zajac says: "When I say selective, I also mean that when there's something you like, you buy it. And remember," he adds, "you can always scale down, but you can never scale up." When they travel, they nearly always come back with new treasures.

Left *"We always think it is much better to have a lot of something,"* say decorators Edward Zajac and Richard Callahan. *Such as mirrors, perhaps – which dominate their apartment, throwing out a sense of reflected light and space.*

Right *The mirrors make the most of the incredibly careful placing of everything in the room. There is nothing of the haphazard here; they explain that they spend a great deal of time on the details of a scheme, and it shows.*

Below *Like most decorator collectors, they find it hard not to collect wherever they are. The chandelier came from Palm Beach, the fireplace – mica cast in clear polyurethane and with the look of rock crystal – was designed by them for a showcase house.*

There is a practical advantage to this aspect of the decorator's collecting passion. The problems and practicalities of arranging and shipping bulky or fragile objects from overseas are commonplace for them; they do not hold the same panic-inducing worries and fears that they do for those of us less involved with the day-to-day business of interior decoration.

They actually have a problem of not buying – they are inveterate collectors of everything from every culture and period. "We buy something we like, when we see it, because we know we can always place it. We become interested in one thing – like Imari porcelain – and then we buy a lot of it. We always think that it is much better to have a lot of something." And they certainly do – every surface is covered with the fruits of their collecting. The fringed shelves of a bookcase hold not only books, but also a miniature room complete with finely detailed furniture; on a green glass console table (designed by Zajac), an eighteenth-century German clock is flanked by glass lamps made from decanters, glass candlesticks, and a cheerfully grinning oriental figure. But every part of every

"a picture should not disappear into the surroundings or be chosen to go with the curtains – it is there to be seen and to disturb"

group seems very much in place for, as they say, "whatever else, a collection must always be part of a design."

This skill of arranging a collection is one that the most talented designers and decorators have in abundance, and one that arch arranger and decorator Frédéric Méchiche exemplifies. In his own Paris apartment, he displays both twentieth-century art and other work of much earlier periods. In the Manhattan apartment of his art-collecting clients – a cathedrallike room of double height – he uses this decorator-collector experience wisely to show off to best advantage their

striking contemporary art collection. Above all, it is the grouping that is important; fine pieces shown in the wrong place or in the wrong way will simply be lost. In order to incorporate this collection into its setting, Méchiche has carefully considered the tonal values of each piece, what each means, and how it will balance against others. There is no need to group like with like. It is debatable in any event whether two indifferent pieces from the same period would work together in the way that a raw 1980s painting in startlingly bright hues by American artist Jean-Michel Basquiat does with an antique desk, whose deep and confident lines exactly balance the strong image above it. The colors used to decorate the apartment are not allowed to distract from the art, yet the scheme is neither boring nor dull. In the dining and living rooms, the tones range from pale lilac

Above left *Frédéric Méchiche nearly always favors a subdued palette, but that is not the same as boring. In this Manhattan apartment, the antique furniture is subtly upholstered – this early nineteenth-century daybed is in fine Parma-violet stripes.*

Above center *In the small salon, two large canvases are hung on a mole-colored wall and grounded by the sofa upholstered in almost the same shade of velvet. The use of sensual textiles gives an air of calm to the space.*

Above right *The color palette has an important part in holding together the diversity of art on display here. Without these neutral tones, the paintings on the long wall would clash and fight with each other. Both the sofa and the chair in this room are designed by Méchiche.*

to taupe gray – that wonderful shade known in some quarters as "elephant's breath." Chairs and sofa are upholstered in tones that range from deep charcoal gray to cream, and all the floors are covered with deliberately plain sisal rugs. "I don't like the idea that a picture disappears into the surroundings or that it is chosen to go with the color of the curtains," says Méchiche. "It is there to be seen and to disturb, so I have worked with a subtle palette."

Throughout the apartment pieces are displayed in an unexpected way. Sculptures are set high, often very high, above a set of built-in bookcases. Everywhere each piece is perfectly balanced by the furniture below it. In a hall, a portrait in a silver gilded frame is offset by a fine marble and gilded pier table. In another room, curved chairs upholstered in soft gray balance a heavy structural piece by British contemporary sculptor Rachel Whiteread. Nowhere do the neutral tones detract from the art.

AN INSTINCTIVE ART

Albeit on a smaller scale, it is the nature of the arrangement that also dominates the collections in London of inveterate decorator-collector Hubert Zandberg. His thesis is that collections only look good when arranged in the French tradition. The word *ensemblier* might be more appropriate, and could perhaps be translated as the art of window-dressing rather than that of merely grouping things together. In his very small apartment, Zandberg's collections are everywhere, and much that is preached is practiced. In one corner of the kitchen, for example, pennants,

miniature flags, toy cars, rolls of colored ribbon and a model parakeet are all brought together in an exuberant group, tied together by color, particularly yellow. And in the bathroom, natural objects, photographs, even rolls of toilet paper are black and white.

As Zandberg says: "It is creating a mood that is important. For the French, it is second nature – the art of arranging is particularly appreciated, and there is a place for it. It is true that some people are intimidated by the way that a decorator arranges his collections, but then some people are intimidated by scatter cushions. When you show your collections, it is for you to make up the

rules and devise your own formula. I try to make the elements relate, bringing different objects and areas into context. When I arrange a collection, I tend to theme it so that the point can immediately be seen, but I also think that it is important that the arrangements of collections should not be contrived, too styled. Although you could say that all art is contrived – super-contrived, actually." Zandberg strongly feels that whereas architecture can be learned, as can an understanding of space, a decorator has to have an underlying feeling for the actual art of decoration, because "without that, nothing will come together."

Left *Only a born decorator could arrange such a diversity of objects with such vivacity, and Hubert Zandberg fits the bill. Juxtaposition is the key word – of shape, texture, object, and theme. No surface is left untouched – and it works.*

Right *The bathroom is a textbook example of relating objects to each other. The room is very small, so no color of any description is allowed: everything has to fall within the black and white and neutral decorative scheme.*

Above right *In the most splendid fretwork and crenelated antique cabinet, Emma Hawkins displays a collection of porcelain. Although her profession is that of antique dealer, she can be counted a decorator-collector because of her sure touch and stylish wit.*

Above far right *Sophisticated is the word for the only white room in the apartment of Coorengel and Calvagrac. A wooden statue of St. Joseph stands behind a period sofa upholstered in gray-violet; and a looped-back, gray, unlined silk curtain adds to the sense of a drawing room in 1940's Paris.*

Below right *Agnès Emery cannot help but decorate everything she touches – even a small bathroom on the top floor of her Brussels house. In this room she has used a small collection of blue-and-white antique tiles to hide the plumbing behind a freestanding bathtub.*

Below far right *The same sense of calm order pervades the mirror-lined dining room. Color is so important here: had Emery used, instead of the chosen neutral, a color that was in violent contrast to the tone of the mirrored glass, the room would have felt very disturbing, rather than cool and watery.*

"it's individuality that we like, and we don't follow fashion or trends... we are lucky to be interior designers, because we can work with our passion"

Emma Hawkins, although not strictly speaking a decorator, has the same finely-tuned decorator's sense as Hubert Zandberg. For example, she puts red leather cricket balls into a heavy wooden bowl so that they become a striking artwork. Elsewhere, she arranges good porcelain plates traditionally in a splendid nineteenth-century display cabinet, but then she balances on the cabinet top a stuffed fox and a badger, who from behind the crenelated fretwork seem to mount a permanent guard over the cabinet's contents, looking down disapprovingly at the action below. She has the affinities of a decorator-collector because of her original and unconventional methods of displaying her finds and her refusal to be sidelined and straitjacketed into adopting conventional patterns of display.

The decorator tendencies of Michael Coorengel and Jean Pierre Calvagrac are shown in this throwaway remark by Michael: "When we buy, we go out looking for specific things, but we usually come back with something different – and usually something better." A decorator-collector always buys the best that he sees when he sees it – even if he doesn't need it at the time. "We buy something and we don't have a clue what to do with it," he goes on to say. "I remember when I was young, I used to search for small things that I liked to make my room nicer. My mother would send me shopping for bread or milk, and next to the grocer's there was a shop that sold knickknacks and plastic things, and I would often buy something from there instead." Neither Coorengel nor Calvagrac have any desire to collect mass-produced objects. "It's not that they are particularly ugly, but it has more to do with a reaction against modern life – the way that people are forced to dress and eat and live in a certain manner. It's individuality that we like, and we don't like to follow fashion or trends. We are lucky to be in interior design because we are able to work with our passion."

WORKING WITH DESIGN

Another interior designer-collector whose work is her passion is renowned Belgian designer, Agnès Emery. "Yes, I have a lot of work, but it is what I want to do," she maintains. A professor of architecture, she not only designs interiors, but also everything to go inside them – tiles, ceramics, textiles, metal furniture and accessories, including exuberant, baroque chandeliers ("a distraction," she calls them), as well as a line of paint colors to tie everything together. Her entire, soaring house is a repository of collections large and small, all based on color – her own mixes, of course.

This is the decorator-collector at her most natural: it would be simply impossible for her not to arrange her possessions with consummate style. In the kitchen, for example, is a collection of ceramics, some designed by her, some variously acquired. In varying blue-green glazes, they are set against a background of azure and aqua, translated into tiles, paint, and wood. Upstairs, a small collection of Japanese prints, many bathed in that particular rich Japanese blue, is hung on a wall painted an even richer blue; and at the top of

Above right *In Charles de Selliers'
kitchen, decorated by Agnès
Emery, water-colored tiles have
been employed above the sink,
and ceramics in interesting
glazes make a fine display.*

Center right *In the de Selliers
living room, on a low table
designed by Emery, a small
flock of wire birds strut their
stuff, underneath a flying
member of the flock.*

Below right *In the kitchen is a
symphony of ceramic and glass,
along which the eye travels
lightly. A high-tailed glass bird
is next to a pumpkin-shaped
crackle-glaze pot and assorted
bowls designed by Emery.*

Above *Every corner of Agnès
Emery's kitchen is like a
painting. The panels of a kitchen
cupboard are lined with tiles
designed and made by Emery;
the wall color tones with the
1930's green of the cupboard;
and the pots on top relate to the
door color.*

Right *An underwater room is
such that one would feel little
surprise were a school of fish to
dart past. The wall is clad with
tiles from Emery's own line and
the work surface below is also
tile-finished. The ceramics,
again mostly by Emery, are both
ornamental and practical.*

the house is a collection of rich robes, made by Agnès from
fabrics in her Eastern textile collection, and used by her as
both clothing and as decoration.

One of her clients, Charles de Selliers, has an eccentric
collection of objects, which were a challenge to display. To
show them in a sympathetic light, Agnès Emery has taken all
these disparate pieces and grouped them in new ways, with
reference to new thought processes. She uses color and scale to
make striking tableaux of what, if left on their own, might
pass unnoticed or, at any rate, unappreciated. To do this, she
has mixed the Selliers collection of ceramics with her own
pieces in her favorite colors of blues, greens, and prunes. She
has added her bold and subtle wall colors – green with sage,
watery green, blue-green and forest green; and purple, lilac,
lavender, eggplant, and prune. Her enormous metal

David Gill just collects pieces that he really wants, rather than searching for huge numbers of any one item. His miniature pieces cannot really be classified, but are just pretty objects that he displays with great charm, allowing each piece enough space and air to show off its individuality. He uses color and shape as links: small tables throughout his apartment are used for their background colors as foils for his little exquisites. From his very first buy —an ivory box on which he spent all his allowance as a schoolboy – he has always enjoyed the allure of the minute. He has only ever wanted to collect things that he is happy to live with, which encourages the massing of miniature pieces that can be packed all the better into his apartment. Unlike a perfectionist collector such as Vicente Wolf, David Gill does not collect in categories, nor does he opt for "important" or even antique pieces as such. What interests him has more to do with the contrast of textures and unusual shapes, and the depths of color and tone of ceramics, metal and wood. All have a place as long as they are deemed "interesting."

collectors have always loved miniature representations of the familiar and the everyday – scale reproductions in wonderful and elaborate detail

or three hundred pounds for a fine collection. Even if you know nothing about them, as you study them in all their intricate detail, you begin to understand the skill and art in portraying not only the features, but also the spirit of the proud commissioning patrons.

Collectors have always loved miniature representations of the familiar and everyday, such as the now highly sought-after scale models of furniture that eighteenth-century cabinet-makers made to advertise their range of designs. And today there are craftspeople making wonderfully detailed scale pieces of elaborate furniture, which sell for many hundreds of pounds to dollhouse collectors. Edward Zajac and Richard Callahan have an evocative miniature room, complete with gilded chairs, urns on pedestals, and draped wall hangings, for example. Charles Paget Wade – who said of himself that he was a child who never grew up – commissioned a craftsman to make scale models of many of the regional farm carts that could be then found in Britain. Throughout the house these tiny, perfect farm wagons are ranged, an exercise in nostalgia and art. This illustrates the appeal of many miniatures, which are small-scale renditions of large-scale beauty, but ones that can be conveniently, if metaphorically, put in the pocket.

Far left *Charles Paget Wade's commissioned collection of local farm wagons is typical of the fascination people have always had with miniature representations. From cars to furniture, models are still made to cater to an eager audience.*

Below left *Man has always had a fascination with the ovoid – witness the fabled eggs made by Peter Carl Fabergé in imperial Russia. David Gill pairs two eggs within handling distance of the onlooker; the instinct with a sphere is always to pick it up.*

Below *Many people today collect dollhouses and miniature furniture, some of which is very expensive. Messrs. Zajac and Callahan have their own miniature room set within a bookcase, furnished in eighteenth-century style.*

FASHIONS IN PORCELAIN

Porcelain has always been widely collected. It was first
introduced into Europe in the seventeenth century; prior to
that, eating dishes were generally utilitarian – wood or
earthenware for the masses and metal plate for the wealthy.
The first pieces made in this new, delicate material,
handpainted with glaze in exotic patterns and designs, were
imported into Europe, particularly Holland, from China.
Because this porcelain was available in Holland in greater
quantities than anywhere else, the Dutch initiated a fashion for
displaying the pieces by massing them in crowded, formal
arrangements. Germany also embraced the new fashion: a
print of Schloss Charlottenburg in Berlin in about 1703 shows
a mirrored porcelain cabinet with pieces grouped in geometric
arrangements around the walls. There were vases on brackets
bordering mirrored panels; platters making a frieze; vases in
molding; and jars on the ground. The fashion reached England
early, of course: in 1652, Evelyn reported supping with Lady
Gerrard, where "all the vessels, which were innumerable, were
of porcelain, she having the most ample and richest collection
of that curiosity in England."

A hundred years later, fine porcelain was no longer just
imported, but was also being made on home ground by
craftsmen such as Josiah Wedgwood, who commissioned
designs from many of the great artists of the day. Pieces were

Above far left *The fine detail is striking in this group of two Parian figures delicately touched with gold and enamel colors, which stand on either side of a fine Worcester porcelain moon flask with pâte-sur-pâte decoration, attributed to William Poynton.*

Above left *Michael Coorengel and Jean Pierre Calvagrac make sure that even their table is laid with decorative art of a rare beauty. Here, an almost harlequin set of china – anything as long as it is gold and white – is grouped with golden glass goblets on a simple wooden table.*

Left *Coral has a strange, almost artificial beauty, so it does not seem odd that Coorengel and Calvagrac have chosen to plant a piece in a tiny, but formal, swagged and gilded urn and stand. It is displayed on a whiter-than-white table.*

Above left *As is the case for nearly every other collection, the miniature looks at its best when displayed en masse. In Hunt Slonem's studio, Parian busts and figures are huddled at one end of a table, waiting for the dance to begin.*

Above right *In the Codman family home in Massachusetts, the dining-room ornament is displayed exactly as it would have been a hundred and fifty years ago, down to the "suitable" still life – in this case, a seventeenth-century painting by Willem Claesz.*

eagerly collected and new designs commissioned by many. There are contemporary accounts of London ladies – not so unlike their counterparts today – visiting Mr. Wedgwood's London shop on a regular basis to see what new novelties, in the way of boxes, dishes, figures, and vases, might be on view. China rooms or cabinets were common among the rich, who might alter their houses to accommodate the new fashion, or build on specific new rooms. In 1799, Mrs. Lybbe Powys reported thus, with perhaps a certain degree of boredom: "Lady Hardy and I went to Blenheim to see the new china-rooms. They are not in the house, but built just after you enter the park, four little rooms fill'd with all sorts of old china... The whole has a pretty effect, but to others might be more amusing than to Lady Hardy and myself as each of us has most of the same sort." In the nineteenth century, china was often displayed on walls, often combined with pictures, as it is in the dining room of the Ogden Codman house.

Many present-day collectors, even those who are not prominently described as miniaturists, are interested in small-scale treasures. There are so many areas to specialize in – from Emma Hawkins' display plates to Coorengel and Calvagrac's neoclassical figures. Hunt Slonem has devoted part of a room to his miniature Parian busts, which have a charm that their larger counterparts cannot achieve; clustered closely together on a deep green cloth, like a group of gossiping schoolgirls, they gaze at a bowl of shells almost as pretty as themselves.

Above left *Diane de Clercq is an artist as well as a designer. These small scraps of thin cardboard are designs that she has painted and then cut into basic sweater shapes, an ongoing example of living art.*

Center left *A single silver hand represents a relatively new collecting passion for Vicente Wolf. Yet the associations have already been made, as is seen in the hand that reaches out from the photograph above.*

Below left *Examples from Diane de Clercq's collection of buttons include some designed by her, matching her painted design stripes, and some African ceramic ones, exuberant and full of life.*

Right *In this diminutive part of a collection of enameled buttons made in Paris by the company Albert Parent in the nineteenth century, the eye is drawn toward the exquisite designs and colors.*

Far right *Miniature collections must be carefully displayed. Various parts of crucifixes, none complete, are gathered closely together by Vicente Wolf, so that the message behind the fragments is at once clear.*

MINUTIAE OF LIFE

Ornament to do with fashion has long been collected, including buttons, which are looked on as a craft of the highest order and were often given as highly prized gifts. In inventories of Queen Elizabeth I's wardrobe and gifts, sets of buttons are often mentioned, fashioned as animals or flowers, often in gold and set with pearls, rubies, and emeralds. Fashion designer Diane de Clercq collects buttons: "Everything I collect comes through painting and design, and I love buttons; they are miniatures of design." In her studio is a chest where literally hundreds of buttons are roughly sorted,

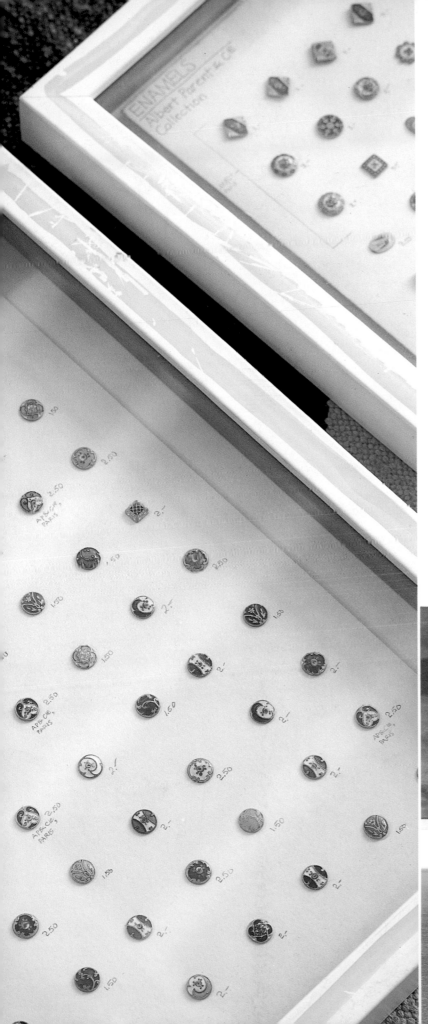

according to type. There are ceramic buttons, enamel buttons, striped buttons, flowered buttons, and buttons with zigzags painted onto them. These are buttons with brio, with attitude, which really do sum up the charm of the miniature.

Displaying the miniature is not as straightforward as it might seem, because it is all too easy to lose the point of a collection if the pieces are grouped too closely or too near to pieces on a larger scale. Vicente Wolf delights in the miniature and knows exactly how to show it to best advantage; around his loft are various small groups of tiny things, sometimes not seen until you are almost upon them. There is a collection of hands, for example, which, he says, "just happened; I saw the silver hand at a dealer's and I bought it, and then I found others and then I realized I had a collection. Wonderful collections are never premeditated, they just evolve. Collections should always be shown together, particularly if they are small things; otherwise, there is a danger of them appearing merely as bric-a-brac. It is a fine line – I think that you have to see them not as decorative objects, but as a point of view, and for that they have to be shown *en masse*." That is certainly true of his small collection of religious images – mostly fragments of different crucifixes – which are arranged closely together on a table so that one looks down on them On a wall or mantelpiece they would have far less meaning. On a shelf, oriental and western figures of varying heights stand close together, framed, as it were, on either side by two black-and-white photographs to give them definition. On

"I think that interiors need a bit of a twist... most have no sense of irony or of real life, and there is nothing harmonious or soulful"

another table, some small moving figures are arranged in such a way that they seem to be running a circuit around the perimeter.

Pieces in miniature can look very good grouped together even if there is no immediate connection between them. However, there must be, at the very least, a decorative link – perhaps that each item is in monochrome or of a certain shape. Hubert Zandberg groups miniatures very well, which is lucky, since his whole apartment is as small as a princeling's cabinet of curiosities and is crammed with things on every surface. "When you show a collection, it is up to you to make up the rules," declares Zandberg. His undoubted skill as a decorator and an arranger means that all his miniature life is very well displayed indeed. Almost every surface, horizontal and vertical, is used as a background for a tiny still life – from

the toy cars attached to the wall to the natural set pieces, such as his collection of horn and bone beakers, bowls, and balls, combined with pieces of the materials in their natural state. "I think," he says, "that interiors need a bit of a twist. Most have no sense of irony and too often there is no sense of real life, nothing harmonious or soulful."

Emma Hawkins shows how even within a traditional setting collections of miniatures can stand out in a fresh and witty way. Wood-turned treen, for example, always seemed to me about as dull as the art of hemming handkerchiefs, until I saw how Emma Hawkins has displayed her own small group. On a glass shelf against a background of polished wood, your eye is sharply drawn to the equally glowing wood of the treen pieces so that you notice and admire their art and craft in fine detail. She is also the only person I have ever met who can give

Right *The joy of the miniature is the sheer fun and fantasy in grouping pieces together. Sometimes, as on this tabletop, it can be simply a pleasing group in terms of proportion and balance.*

Below right *On other occasions it is simplicity that works best. In Vicente Wolf's Manhattan-view apartment, a line of bottles – more than ten and not just green – are lined up on a windowsill, where they catch the light and show off their various shapes and tones.*

Far right *The links in this display are not immediately apparent; there is an ethnic theme, certainly, but also a more mathematical connection between objects, based on shape, texture, and proportion. The dark tones of the solid pieces are set off by the glass dish of apples.*

Above left *There is real movement in this group of miniature figures. Instead of arranging them in serried ranks, Vicente Wolf has set them out on a marble tabletop to run and win a race. The silver candle base acts as a necessary balance to their limited proportions.*

Above right *These are nut-crackers, certainly, but generally not as you know them. Finely carved in wood, this collection ranges from turned, almost treenlike pieces of simple and elegant design to grotesque, novelty pieces so loved in the nineteenth century.*

a collection of wooden corkscrews real charm; and she is equally successful with her collection of tiny, fragile birds' skulls – twenty or so – which she has grouped together on a polished wooden table, where they look for all the world like beautiful chess pieces.

Miniaturists do, without question, love their tiny collections, which can be very involving: every time you bend to inspect or study, the proud collector will nearly always explain the finer points of each piece – often at some length. Perhaps this is because a collection of small pieces is somehow more personal than one of large objects. Many of the small items can be picked up, handled, and admired at close quarters, and this invites a particular intimacy. For these reasons, a collection of miniature pieces is a good area for the novice collector to choose. Easily portable, easy to get to know, they often pave the way to greater collecting heights.

Above left *Some people may find them distasteful, but for many others there is a real beauty in these tiny, fragile bird skulls, each one complete in every delicate detail and as intricate as the most finely carved piece of ivory.*

Left *Although as a hobby today the collecting and cataloguing of butterflies might be frowned on, in the nineteenth century it was considered an admirable pastime. Shells, too, have long been collected by ladies of leisure and men of science.*

Right *Laid out here, and looking rather like miniature medieval instruments of some mysterious torture, is Emma Hawkins's interesting collection of treen. The literal definition of treen is simply 'made of tree', but the word is generally used to describe small objects made from turned wood.*

THE ART OF DISPLAY

The art of collecting is closely linked to that of display. The ways in which to achieve the best effects by putting a collection on view are important parts of the process. With the exception of King Midas and the odd dragon guarding hidden caches of fabled jewels, most people want their collections to be admired and enjoyed by others. A collection should not be hidden in boxes and behind doors, as even the most modest is enhanced by being shown in the best possible light, where its importance can be viewed by all.

In the past, displaying a collection to advantage was for many the first demonstration of an interest in interior decoration – of the wish to make a house and its contents look beautiful as well as functional. The great collectors of the seventeenth and eighteenth centuries housed their collections in various ways. Small, valuable pieces – tiny jewellike paintings and miniatures, boxes, small decorative objects – were often kept together in proportionately small rooms, often described as closets or cabinets, where their fine details could be appreciated at close hand. Larger rooms were designed to house the fabulously popular oriental blue-and-white porcelain exported from the Far East; and even larger objects, such as sculpture and paintings, were housed in purpose-built galleries, either within the house or as important architectural additions. When architect Robert Adam remodeled Syon House in Brentford, England, for the Percy family in the 1760s, at each end of a long gallery he created two small closets: a circular one in which porcelain was to be displayed and a square one designed for the display of miniatures.

As far as the manner of display itself is concerned, seventeenth-century collectors probably hung their paintings far higher than we would now – usually almost to ceiling height, and often against a background of richly colored, figured silk or wool. These elevated pictures would usually be canted forward for ease of view. Eighteenth-

Far left *At Snowshill Manor, Wade paid careful attention to the arrangement and display of his many and various collections, grouping items into coherent stories. This room, "Admiral," contains nautical things, including a collection of naval swords.*

Left *This display in Françoise De Nobele's Parisian apartment is a real cabinet of curiosities in the seventeenth-century sense. A fascination with the natural is apparent, as is a certain discipline, with sea life on the lower shelf, other curios above.*

Below left *This is a perfectly structured composition. Height is supplied by the picture set in its studded neoclassical frame; depth is added with the urn flanked by figures of the young Queen Victoria and the then Duke of Kent.*

Below right *In this room celebrating the romantic allure of Europe in the late eighteenth and early nineteenth centuries, the neoclassical ceramics are complemented by fine pieces of furniture, such as a William IV rosewood table and English and French side tables and cabinets.*

century collections were often hung in symmetrical ranks, apparently designed to be an integral part of the formal architectural scheme rather than making a display devised for easy viewing of the pictures. In the nineteenth century, a Gothic setting, a particularly popular decorative style at the time, often seemed particularly appropriate to collectors of antiquities. They also used old wood to give an early Renaissance look; venerable was the desired effect, although how venerable antlers, old suits of armor, and weapons such as swords, axes, and shields were is open to debate.

CONTEMPORARY DISPLAY

Today we are just as particular as we were then about the way in which pictures should be hung and objects displayed, although, along with every other aspect of interior decoration, our tastes have understandably changed. Perhaps there are not as many suits of armor standing in the turn of a stair, or plates lined neatly above the picture rail, but the display of a collection is still an integral part of the whole collecting experience. Taste is so subjective that it can be a trap for the collector. Displaying a collection is not about fashionable taste as it is understood in a decorative sense; rather, it transcends perceived conceptions of style and sets its own. Yet the manner in which a collection is displayed does add hugely to its appeal or lack of it. There can be no comparison between a collection of dusty objects stored in a cupboard out of sight and those same

objects arranged artfully, stylishly, and cleverly throughout a living space.

The same basic rules apply to the display of objects as they do to interior decoration in general, and to the arrangement of rooms in particular. A room – indeed the whole house – should be planned so that all the elements are in proportion, in scale, and in harmony with each other, and the theory is just the same for a collection. Franck Delmarcelle and Laurent Dombrowicz are aware of the rules and take the display of their varied collections very seriously. "When we see an object, we tend to know where it will go best; it is instinctive," they explain. "Sometimes we have to change its place, but we are rather loath to do that. We take great care with our display; each piece must be added in the right conjunction with the others, and each must be seen in the right light, and in harmony. They are visual compositions, and this is where much of the pleasure is to be gained."

Left *In a Manhattan apartment designed and decorated by Frédéric Méchiche, his successful conjunction of the antique and the modern is evident. Two subtle, velvet-upholstered chairs are furnished with cushions in the same tones as the art.*

Above right *Vicente Wolf is not only good at displaying each collection, he is also good at combining styles and periods in a seamless, pleasing way. An antique gilded table, a twentieth-century black leather upholstered chair, and photographs and buddhas work elegantly together.*

Above far right *In Pennsylvania, Polly Dickens and Mark Gilbey have arranged their living room in the simplest and most stylish of ways. Grouped together are small collections of silver and glass, displayed as an integral part of the design.*

Below right *In Jerry and Susan Lauren's Manhattan apartment, the collection of weathervanes, although displayed to be noticed, is an integral part of the room. The furniture has deliberately been kept low-key and simple, upholstered in pristine white.*

Below far right *In Vicente Wolf's apartment, less is less: simple, oversized shapes are grouped together, with no decorative distraction – the curtainless window and the sofabed without hangings, which was designed by Wolf.*

GROUPING OBJECTS

Two of the most influential young designers in Paris today – Michael Coorengel and Jean Pierre Calvagrac – know this well. Their apartment is arranged throughout so that the objects they have chosen are displayed in such a way that each piece can shine within a disciplined and integrated group. Michael Coorengel explains: "When you group things, they have a stronger impact on the room. In any room, if everything were merely set out in lines, there would be no charm or atmosphere; putting them together in small groups creates intimate corners. It must look almost as a picture – each corner should be complete in itself." There should be a discipline within the grouping and in its position in a room. Space between the objects is also important, as is their visual balance. Coorengel and Calvagrac decided on a particular discipline: "The criterion that we use is the shape of the group – it is always a triangle, based on the perfection of the pyramid. We then compose our display from the base to the top of the triangle. We don't

do it on purpose – we don't go around saying 'where's the triangle?' – but a shape like that makes it easier to read, even if you don't know why."

Groups can come in many forms; some collections, for example, lend themselves to being grouped quite, or very, closely together. This obviously applies to collections of small objects whose impact might so easily be lost if they were scattered too freely. They may all be of the same genre, as is Hubert Zandberg's wondrous collection of pennants, objects that in another context would frankly have very little impact at all. Grouped together tightly on the wall, the pennants make a lively, amusing, and original picture. Peter Hone's collection of seals is yet another example of how to show small objects: these perfect miniature pieces are often unappreciated because each example is too subtle to arrest the eye when seen in isolation; yet seen massed together against a white-painted wall, they draw that eye irresistibly.

In Paul Dawson and Harold Galloway's kitchen is a large collection of nineteenth-century relief-molded pitchers. They are from

Above left *This is a perfect example of Coorengel and Calvagrac's rules of grouping: a decorative vignette is put together following a triangular pattern, starting from a deep base and rising, through a coral-filled glass flask, to the top of the obelisk behind.*

Above right *These glass pieces bear out artist Hunt Slonem's theory that anything looks better when displayed as part of a group; they are disparate in shape, but united in their colorful hues to make an effortless, but striking, display.*

Opposite *Control and discipline are needed when so many different objects are grouped so closely together. An inspection of this montage of pennants and flags, which stretches over two walls, reveals a unity of color, as well as a careful combination of shapes.*

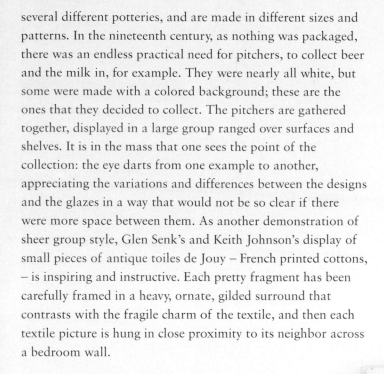

several different potteries, and are made in different sizes and patterns. In the nineteenth century, as nothing was packaged, there was an endless practical need for pitchers, to collect beer and the milk in, for example. They were nearly all white, but some were made with a colored background; these are the ones that they decided to collect. The pitchers are gathered together, displayed in a large group ranged over surfaces and shelves. It is in the mass that one sees the point of the collection: the eye darts from one example to another, appreciating the variations and differences between the designs and the glazes in a way that would not be so clear if there were more space between them. As another demonstration of sheer group style, Glen Senk's and Keith Johnson's display of small pieces of antique toiles de Jouy – French printed cottons, – is inspiring and instructive. Each pretty fragment has been carefully framed in a heavy, ornate, gilded surround that contrasts with the fragile charm of the textile, and then each textile picture is hung in close proximity to its neighbor across a bedroom wall.

This page *On a mantelpiece, a collection of treasured objects, from family photographs to drawings and small unusual objects of varying shapes, is sparingly arranged. It is the horizontal progression that is so effective here – the way the eye is drawn along from one piece to the next.*

Above left *One of the most effective ways of showing off a collection is to group the pieces close together, although proportion and scale must still be taken into account. A perfect example is Glen Senk and Keith Johnson's innovative display of framed toile de Jouy fragments.*

Below left *Paul Dawson and Albert Galloway have built up a fine collection of William de Morgan lusterware plates and platters, all designed by him, but executed by assistants. Although each piece is wonderful on its own, their impact when grouped together like this is far greater.*

Above right *A coherent and pleasing group has been made from these pieces of ivory collected by Peter Hone. Much care has been taken in the distribution of shapes upon the marble-topped chest-of-drawers, which dates from the French Empire period.*

Below right *On a sideboard, nineteenth-century Staffordshire relief-molded pitchers, with similar background colors, are displayed. The central piece commemorates the death of Prince Albert, and its handle is made up of his many honors. Behind is an unusual stoneware waterfilter by Doulton.*

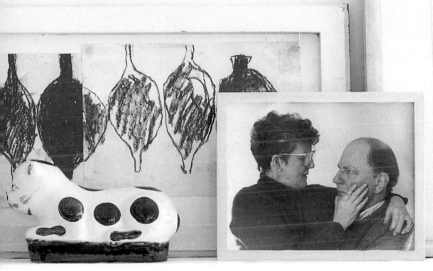

Above left *An intricate group is arranged by Emma Hawkins on a glass table. A connecting theme of material, bone and ivory is expanded and enlarged by her choice of objects – an intricately carved box, a small bust and an early set of flatware. In every direction is something to ponder.*

Above right *It is always worth putting on display the smallest of objects – often miniature beauty is the finest. Here three unrelated objects have been put together on a mottled grey background with due regard to the shape that each one makes in the whole arrangement.*

Right *The most adaptable of materials, bone and horn, have been used through the centuries to make both functional and decorative objects of every description. Here, on a natural background, Hubert Zandberg has grouped together many examples of handmade artifacts, each one unique.*

BACKGROUND DESIGNS

Tightly packed displays should also be created when a collection is composed of pieces made of one material – silver, tortoiseshell, bone, or ivory, perhaps – but where those pieces are varied in content, shape, and design. Grouped closely, the individual pieces have a cohesion that they might otherwise lack. The background is also important here; Peter Hone displays his collection of ivory pieces on a dark wood bureau, and Hubert Zandberg does the opposite, subtly laying everything out on a natural linen cloth. Certainly, neither collector accepts a mediocre middle line when designing his display.

Hunt Slonem, artist that he is, breaks for the border of the acceptable grouping. "If you buy enough of anything, even if some of it is hideous, when it is put all together it looks wonderful," he maintains. The method is amply demonstrated in his enormous studio, where most things are grouped *en masse* – in his case, this means much masse. A collection of glass candlesticks, for example, is crowded along a refectory table. At different heights and of different designs,

they are not necessarily pairs; in fact, the majority of them are single examples, but the impact they make is accentuated by their being arranged artlessly, bent candles and all, in higgledy-piggledy fashion.

Large objects require a different solution. Whether they are shown together or separately, they must be given enough air around them to breathe freely; crammed too closely together, they get lost and cease to have individual relevance. Each of the large photographs collected by Vicente Wolf is framed simply and given plenty of surrounding space against white walls. The same principle lies behind Laurent Dombrowicz and Franck Delmarcelle's arrangement of statues of angels and other uplifting figures. Carefully positioned throughout the house, they are seen as individual pieces, yet connect with each other and with the other grouped collections.

Large-scale pieces must also be balanced with other pieces or groups of equal weight and proportions. This formula is adopted by Jerry and Susan Lauren for their weather-vanes, which are counterbalanced by the simple, yet strong, contemporary furniture that decorates their apartment.

SOLO STARS

Every rule – particularly in interior decoration – is made to be broken. Not every collection should necessarily be displayed *en groupe*; some collections are more striking when displayed in relative (and this word is important) isolation. Strong pieces to which the eye is instantly drawn are often better displayed as integral parts of a scheme, but as single items standing alone within it. With an unerring artist's eye, David Gill arranges even his own apartment as if it were a gallery, allowing each piece and each object to be seen as unique, to be sampled at leisure and appreciated on its own as well as a part of the greater whole.

Vicente Wolf's collection of Buddhas is not displayed in a group together; instead, each Buddha is seen in splendid isolation. One will be discovered sitting placidly along a corridor and another is placed around a corner, where it is met unexpectedly, almost as if each were in a different shrine along a pilgrim's way.

Were they to be shown together, they would lose their individual impact, have less of an air of mystery. Frédéric Méchiche, too, in the Manhattan apartment he has decorated and arranged to hold a client's important twentieth-century art collection, has emphasized the individual strengths of every work, placing each one in intelligent juxtaposition to the other pieces. He has also – and this is difficult – incorporated into the scheme some fine pieces of antique furniture, arranging them in the same manner so each item can be appreciated not only for itself, but also for the way in which it works with the art displayed around it. The correct use of scale is important here – vital, in fact, when dealing with works of such strength. In complete contrast to such high profile pieces, Glen Senk and Keith Johnson's large utilitarian objects, such as gates and radiators, are displayed like treasures in an art gallery, standing alone, surrounded by space and backed by simple white walls.

Left *In the Codman house, many of the heavy, mid-Victorian decorative ideas were swept away at the end of the nineteenth century. Light and space were essential when displaying treasures.*

Above right *Vicente Wolf collects orchids, as well as figures of Buddha. Here, the timeless hand of the Buddha is juxtaposed with the fragile beauty of a plant with a finite life.*

Above far right *Should you happen to collect radiators, you might well wonder what would be the best way to display them. Look no further: Glen Senk and Keith Johnson know that splendid isolation is the answer.*

Center right *A bust of George Stephenson, engineer and maker of The Rocket, the famous British steam engine, has been placed by Peter Hone in solitary splendor on a pile of books.*

Center far right *In Jerry and Susan Lauren's hallway, a fine quilt of about 1800, made from a variety of block- and roller-printed cottons, hangs behind a noble nineteenth-century copper ram, making an encircling, triumphal garland.*

Below right *In the Lauren apartment, a grotesque "Devil" pitcher, made around 1930, is displayed on a plinth so that every aspect can be admired. Close by on another is a carved wooden teashop trade figure in polychrome and gilt.*

Below far right *Vicente Wolf takes an evocative photograph, mounts it simply but dramatically, and displays it on a chair whose metal curves emphasize the stark treatment of the photo.*

Above far left *Like an ancient Greek chorus, this small but enchanting group of glass and ceramics has been placed by Polly Dickens in such a way that the finer points of each piece can be seen and appreciated, and the most is made of both color and texture.*

Below far left *Hunt Slonem is never one for the tentative gesture; like the pieces in one of those blindfold parlor games where the object must be identified by its texture, he has put together a group of contrived contrast.*

Left *For Hubert Zandberg, the fun of arranging objects is in the juxtaposition. Here is one of his more complex pictures of texture – hot and cold, rough and smooth. Carved wood, checkered quills, smooth spheres, and a woven nest are a complete natural history lesson at one swoop.*

TEXTURES AND CONTRASTS

Grouping pieces by common texture or by their contrasting different textures is also an important display device. This is not the same as keeping together a collection of ivory or silver; rather, it is using different textures to give a resonance similar to that of an interior decoration scheme in which hard is combined with soft, or cool with hot. Hubert Zandberg and Hunt Slonem are past masters at this texture game. Zandberg likes to make a textural picture with his displays – horn might be combined with wood, shells, and leather, for example. He says that "the fun is the juxtaposition – the putting together of the metal and wood." Slonem, on the other hand, builds up textures in the same way that he might approach an artwork. A still life of part of his collection might contain shells combined with busts and sculptural pieces in plaster, marble, and china, each slightly different in texture – some reflective, some matte – and each element adding interest to its neighbor.

Although displaying a collection based on the work of one person – lamps by the American glassmaker Louis Comfort Tiffany, perhaps – can be monotonous, it can be very effective if the designs and patterns are subtle and varied enough. This sort of signature grouping usually works best with smaller pieces, such as ceramics or silver. For example, brightly colored twentieth-century pottery, such as that designed for Carlton Ware or Clarice Cliff, always looks best grouped together. When these collections are studied together, pleasure comes from seeing both the differences and the similarities exposed in proximity.

Above left *These charming and delicate pieces of Whitefriars and Walsh glass, including a decanter and a flask designed by T.G. Jacks in the early 1870s, are shown at their best in an ebonized parcel-gilt cabinet attributed to the designer Christopher Dresser.*

Above center *Agnès Emery is known for her use of color when arranging collections, but she is also confident when using no color at all. In this room, everything is black, white, or of metal. It takes a committed mind to classify books through color rather than subject.*

THEMATIC DISPLAYS

One of the most effective ways of displaying a collection is to group together by theme. This may be period, as with Paul Dawson and Harold Galloway's fine collection of all things Victorian, a broad theme that they then break down into smaller categories. It might be color, function or, perhaps, material. In Dawson and Galloway's treasure-filled house, many of the rooms themselves have a theme, such as "The Englishman Abroad," a room in which every picture is a nineteenth-century landscape painted in Europe by a luminary such as Edward Lear. The

subject of another room is the Aesthetic Movement, where the decoration is like the inside of a hatbox. One room is devoted to Whitefriars glass, the relative simplicity of which was inspired by the art critic John Ruskin's antagonism to the "unnaturalness" of the cut-glass designs that were popular in the nineteenth century.

Color is the key to successful interior decoration, so it is often also the answer to displaying a collection with brio. Belgian decorator Agnès Emery is the queen of color and uses it as an important display tool. In her hands, pieces that might otherwise pass unnoticed evolve into harmonious

Above right *In the house of Charles de Selliers, Agnès Emery has certainly used color as a link. Everything is sea-rich green – from floor tiles to painted cabinet, walls, and floor lamps. The swimming fish look perfectly at home.*

groups and striking tableaux, linked by color. In the house of a client, she has transformed a collection of pieces that might otherwise descend into kitsch by arranging them into eye-catching, color-based groups. Against a deep green wall, and on a green and cream checkerboard floor, a pair of ornate carved floor lamps with green figured velvet shades flank a green painted chest, on which is a trio of grotesque green ceramic fish. The effect is stylish and witty – and very effective.

It is worth considering whether, taking into account that most true collectors rarely stop at only one interest, a collection can ever be

displayed in tandem with other things – with everyday objects or with the components of another collection. Many people with several collections find, consciously or unconsciously, that there is a link between the different areas of interest. Jerry and Susan Lauren, for example, combine their collection of the arts and crafts of America with another of Native American and Caribbean art, some of which is contemporary. In this case, the link between the collections is a certain naivety of design that applies as much to children's toy cars and trucks as it does to antique weathervanes and a particular style of modern art. Because

Left *On the basis that the aesthetic tastes of a collector will affect everything he chooses, the most sophisticated of collectors combine with ease more than one discipline. Here, Dombrowicz and Delmarcelle group together examples of silvered candlesticks, religious ornament, and animal art.*

Below left *In Jerry and Susan Lauren's apartment, these small, busy models of workaday trucks and vehicles, in all their carefully observed, brightly colored detail, look all the better for being displayed on shelves and between the purity of unadorned glassware.*

Right *By their very contrast, the classical urns complete with hieroglyphs and the silver candlesticks on the shelves of this bureau simply serve to accentuate the strangeness of the bird skeletons and skulls, not to mention the apparently fossilized foot and spiny crab.*

of the design discernment of the Laurens' combined eyes, and also because they are absolutely single-minded in knowing what they like, all the different pieces of their collections work well together.

There are as many different views and ways on how to show off a collection as there are collections themselves. No one way is better than another; it all depends on the size and nature of the particular collection, and on the personality of the collector who has put it together. The only really important thing to remember is that the viewers must be able to perceive that they are indeed looking at a collection, that is, objects put together for a purpose. Whether things are massed closely or scattered throughout the space, there needs to be a relationship between each one of them and a point to their juxtaposition. As Vicente Wolf says: "Collections should always be shown together. You have to see them not as decorative objects, but as a point of view."

Sources and museums

MUSEUM AND GALLERY COLLECTIONS

UK

The larger museum and gallery collections, both in London and in regional centers, can provide the collector with rich sources of exhibits and information in a chosen area. The **Victoria & Albert Museum** (Cromwell Road, South Kensington, SW7 2RL; www.vam.ac.uk) in London, to take but one example, would be invaluable for a collector of architectural metalwork, of nineteenth-century ceramics or of antique costume and textiles – and for almost any other decorative arts category imaginable.

To see the passion of a collector in action, smaller specialist museums and galleries are well worth a visit. In London, **Sir John Soane's Museum** (13 Lincoln's Inn Fields, WC2A 3BP; www.soane.org) was built by the great architect as his own home, where he displayed antiquities and works of art in fascinating style. The Wallace Collection (Hertford House, Manchester Square, W1U 3BN; www.the-wallace-collection.org.uk) displays one of the finest collections of art ever assembled by one family, including French eighteenth-century paintings, porcelain and furniture.

A completely different collecting passion is found at the **Pitt Rivers Museum** (South Parks Road, Oxford OX1 3PP; www.prm.ox.ac.uk). The eponymous Lt.-General was an influential figure in the development of archaeology and evolutionary anthropology, donating his collections to the University of Oxford in 1884.

The Pitt Rivers now has half a million objects, ranging from a Tahitian costume collected by Captain Cook, to magic amulets and charms and tribal masks from around the globe.

USA

The Metropolitan Museum of Art, New York (1000 Fifth Avenue at 82nd Street, New York NY 10028; www.metmuseum.org) is one of the most comprehensive museums in the world with collections of art from cultures around the world and dating from antiquity to modern times. The museums of the **Smithsonian Institution** (www.si.edu) include the American Art Museum, Natural History Museum, and the Cooper-Hewitt National Design Museum among many others.

The **Winterthur Museum, Garden and Library** (Route 52, Winterthur DE 19735; www.winterthur.org) houses a magnificent collection of American antiques in an estate created by Henry Francis du Pont. The **Isabella Stewart Gardner Museum** (280 The Fenway, Boston, MA 02115; www.gardnermuseum.org) is a lovely house that has remained essentially unchanged since Mrs. Gardner's death in 1924, and stands as a testament to her talents as a collector and in displaying her treasured objects.

HISTORIC PROPERTIES

UK

Maintained houses that are open to the public are also excellent places not only for study of the collections themselves, but also for an essence of the collectors who formed them. **The National Trust** (PO Box 39, Bromley, Kent BR1 3XL; www.nationaltrust.org.uk) administers many fine, idiosyncratic and personal collections in houses throughout the UK, including Snowshill Manor (Nr. Broadway, WR12 7JU) featured in this book. The Trust's website gives an option to browse through 'Collections' – listed by categories as diverse as agricultural equipment, musical instruments, silver and toys – that are annotated with details of the properties in which the relevant collections can be found.

Other properties open to the public – independently owned, run by other preservation societies or by local authorities – can be tracked down through the pages of the publications listed here or on the internet.

USA

The Royal Oak Foundation (26 Broadway, Suite 950, New York, NY 10004, www.royal-oak.org) is the US affiliate membership of the British National Trust.

The Society for the Preservation of New England Antiquities (SPNEA, Harrison Gray Otis House, 141 Cambridge Street, Boston MA; www.spnea.org) administers thirty-five properties in New England, dating from the seventeenth century to the present. These include two of the houses featured in this book: Codman House (The Grange, Codman Road, Lincoln, Massachusetts 01733) and Gropius House (68 Baker Bridge Road, Lincoln, Massachusetts 01773).

Historic Hudson Valley (150 White Plains Road, Tarrytown, NY 10591; www.hudsonvalley.org) owns and administers five public properties in the Hudson River Valley dating back to the eighteenth century including Van Cortlandt Manor and Washington Irving's Sunnyside. **The Preservation Society of Newport County** (424 Bellevue Avenue, Newport, RI 02840; www.newportmansions.org) preserves and protects eleven grand Newport mansions including The Breakers and Rosecliff.

AUCTION HOUSES

The auction saleroom is now a global arena, with the major houses staging sales linked by telephone and internet buying. Specialist collectibles sales are therefore, theoretically at least, open to all. The three major world auction houses all have websites with calendars of sales, contact details in various countries, and facilities to buy on line: **Sotheby's** (www.sothebys.com); **Christie's** (www.christies.com); and **Phillips, de Pury & Luxembourg** (www.phillips-auctions.com). Local auctioneers, or specialist ones selling in a particular collecting category, are also best searched out on the internet. The site www.thesaurus.co.uk has facilities to search auction houses throughout the world.

PUBLICATIONS

Museums and Galleries Yearbook, M. Wright (Ed.), published by the Museums Association (ISBN 0902102834) lists UK museums and galleries and specialist bodies and associations.

Art Galleries and Museums of Britain, KGP Publishing (ISBN 0952280795).

The Guide to Art Exhibitions 2001: Great Britain and Ireland, published by Lund Humphries (ISBN 0853317836).

Miller's Collectors' Guides cover an enormous number of collecting areas, from glass of the 1920s and 1930s to postcards and science and technology collectibles. A full range of individual titles is found on the publisher's website: www.reedbooks.co.uk. *Miller's Antique Shops, Fairs & Auctions* has 8000 entries.

Antiques Trade Gazette gives up to-date information about the British antiques trade and dates of up-coming auction sales. It is also available online at www.antiquestradegazette.com.

The Official Museum Directory 2002, Natl Register Pub Co. (ISBN 0872179060) is a weighty and expensive tome listing museums across the US, available in reference libraries.

The Epicurean Collector by Patrick Dunne (ISBN 0821227599) is an entertaining and informative book about collecting culinary antiques.

Museums of the World, published by KG Saur Verlag (ISBN 3598206062) lists 24,624 museums in 191 countries.

The Good Web Guide to Museums & Galleries, Matthew Glanville (ISBN 1903282144) is a neat little reference book to assist internet searches of world museums and galleries.

Index

Author's acknowledgments

Even had I not formed the occasional small collection before embarking upon this book, I certainly would have started at least one after writing it. The enthusiasm of collectors is so infectious, the breadth of individual interests so wide, that one would have to be a dullard not to get caught up in the passion of the collectors we met and talked to. I would like to thank them all very much for giving so generously of their time and knowledge, and for letting us enter, briefly, their world.

I would also like to thank everyone involved in producing the book: Jacqui Small, for the inspiration and encouragement; Simon Upton, who took some wonderful photographs, becoming almost as enthusiastic as me in the process; Nadine Bazar, who painstakingly tracked down our quarry; Judy Spours, for making such perfect sense of all the seemingly unconnected strands; and Ashley Western, for ultimately making the whole thing look so good.

Location acknowledgments

Peter Adler's house in London appears on pages 36, 44, 45 *above left*, 45 *below right*, 94 *right* and 186–7.

An apartment in New York designed by Frédéric Méchiche appears on pages 18, 78–9, 142–3 and 170.

Diane de Clercq's home in Rome appears on pages 1 *right*, 13 *right*, 112–15, 160 *above* and *bottom* and 160–1.

Codman House, a property of the Society for the Preservation of New England Antiquities, appears on pages 50, 52 *below*, 54–7, 136–7, 159 *right*, 178 and 192 *right*.

Michael Coorengel and Jean Pierre Calvagrac's apartment in Paris appears on pages 13 *below left*, 15, 22, 30–3, 45 *above right*, 147 *above*, 158 *right* and 173 *left*.

Laurent Dombrowicz and Franck Delmarcelle's house in Northern France appears on pages 11, 14 *above left*, 34–5, 94 *left*, 95, 128–9, 154, 184 above and 192 *center*.

Agnès Emery's house in Brussels appears on pages 4, 45 *below left*, 108 *right*, 109, 121, 134, 147 *below*, 148–9, 182–3 and 192 *left*.

Mark Gilbey and Polly Dickens' house in Pennsylvania appears on pages 19 *above right* and *below left*, 108 *left*, 171 *above right*, 174, 175 and 180 *above*.

David Gill's house in London appears on page 8 *above right*, 74–5, 116 and 156 *below*.

Walter Gropius House, a property of the Society for the Preservation of New England Antiquities, appears on pages 3, 9 *below left*, 16–17, 58–9, 110–11, 118 and 138–9.

Emma Hawkins' house in Edinburgh appears on pages 52 *right*, 60–1, 82–5, 92–3, 106 *below right*, 146, 163 *above right*, 164–5, 176 *left* and 185.

Peter Hone's apartment in London appears on pages 19 *above left*, 24–9, 155, 169 *below left*, 175 *above* and 179 *center left*.

Reed Krakoff's apartment in New York, designed in collaboration with Pamplemousse Design, appears on pages 14 *above right*, 62–3, 76–7 and 151 *left*.

Jerry and Susan Lauren's apartment in New York appears on page 10–11, 64–9, 171 *below left*, 179 *center right* and *below left* and 184 *below*.

Françoise de Nobele and Jean-Michel Smilenko's apartment in Paris appears on pages 1 *center*, 8 *below right*, 12, 42–3, 86–7, 120, 126–7 and 168–9.

A Regency villa in the south of England appears on pages 9 *right*, 13 *above left*, 17, 53 *left*, 70–3, 88–9, 158 left, 169 *below right*, 174 *below*, 175 *below* and 182.

Charles de Selliers' house in Brussels appears on page 130–3, 149 *right* and 183.

Glen Senk and Keith Johnson's house in Philadelphia appears on page 103–5, 174 *above*, 179 *above right*.

Hunt Slonem's apartment in New York appears on pages 96–7, 102, 102–3, 124–5, 152, 159 *left*, 173 *right* and 180 *below*.

The National Trust, Snowshill Manor, appears on pages 8 *left*, 38–41, 52 *above*, 100, 101, 122–3, 156 *above* and 168 *left*.

Vicente Wolf's apartment in New York appears on pages 48–9, 80–1, 119, 150, 151 *right*, 160 *center*, 161, 162 *left*, 162–3, 163 *above left*, 171 *above left* and *below right*, 176 *right*, 179 *above left* and 179 *below right*.

Charles Worthington's house in Kent appears on pages 1 *left*, 98, 106 *above* and *below left* and 107.

The New York apartment of Edward Zajac and Richard Callahan of A & I Design Partners Inc., appears on pages 9 *above left*, 10, 19 *below right*, 140–1 and 157

Hubert Zandberg's apartment in London appears on pages 2, 14 *below*, 46–7, 90–1, 100–01, 144–5, 172, 177 and 180–1.